D1394913

WHY YOU WON'T GET RICH

WHY YOU WON'T
GET RICH

How Capitalism Broke its
Contract with Hard Work

Robert Verkaik

ONEWORLD

A Oneworld Book

First published by Oneworld Publications in 2021

Copyright © Robert Verkaik 2021

ISBN 978-1-78607-807-0
eISBN 978-1-78607-808-7

Typeset by Geethik Technologies
Printed and bound in Great Britain by Clays Ltd, Elcograf S.p.A.

Oneworld Publications
10 Bloomsbury Street
London WC1B 3SR
England

Stay up to date with the latest books,
special offers, and exclusive content from
Oneworld with our newsletter

Sign up on our website
oneworld-publications.com

MIX
Paper from
responsible sources
FSC® C018072

I wish to dedicate this book to all the volunteers and staff working at Citizens Advice.

Last year more than 20,000 advisers from hundreds of communities gave up their time for free to help 2.8 million people.

In the midst of the 2020 pandemic, which cost many lives and stole so many livelihoods, Citizens Advice, which is a non-political charity, was often the only place people could turn to for help. Its work has never been more vital.

In particular, I wish to say a personal thank you to Ruth, Jan, Juliet, Anna, Cass and Sandra whose knowledge, patience and expertise never cease to amaze. Their work makes the community richer.

CONTENTS

The names of some individuals referred to in this book have been changed. Some of the stories are composite case studies. The cases were all taken from interviews and encounters with the author since 2015.

INTRODUCTION:
THE ROAD TO WEMBLEY

My father-in-law loves to regale us about the time his friend Harry took him along to the FA Cup Final between Arsenal and Liverpool in 1971.

'We worked together. I was an Arsenal fan and he supported Liverpool', the story always begins. Then he continues:

> The week before the final he asked me if I wanted to go with him to Wembley. I had planned to watch the match on television, but it was the final so I said 'Yes, please'. Unbelievably the score was 0-0 at full time so the game went into extra time. First they got one, then we did. When Charlie George scored the amazing winner and went flat on his back I was grinning from ear to ear, but I made sure to turn away from Harry because I could sense how upset he was. I think it was the greatest day of my life.

We're all Arsenal fans in our family and most of us have basic club (Red) membership. In 2017 Arsenal once again got through to the FA Cup Final at Wembley. I had never been to a Wembley final and thought it would be a once-in-a-lifetime treat for my two sons. So I tried to buy three tickets. Arsenal had been allocated 28,000 tickets priced at £45, £65, £85 and £115.[1]

Some of the tickets went to season-ticket holders, some to corporate sponsors and others found their way onto the black market where they were being sold for hundreds of pounds. Ordinary fans hoping for a once-in-a-lifetime experience didn't get a look in.

In 1971 the cost of an FA Cup Final ticket was just £1, which meant most fathers and mothers could afford to treat their children to a day out at Wembley. So nearly 50 years later why couldn't I, a reasonably well-off journalist? The casual arrangement of turning up at Wembley, as described by my father-in-law, is totally unrecognisable. Had inflation taken such a heavy toll on our spending power that in 2017 you needed £45 to watch the same fixture that half a century ago cost £1? Or was I genuinely worse off than my father-in-law when he was my age?

I had to find out.

According to the Office for National Statistics' (ONS) composite price index, which takes account of inflation, the cost of living in 2017 was 1,243.63 percent higher than in 1971.[2] So a pound sterling from 1971 was actually equivalent to the purchasing power of £13.44 in 2017, a difference of just £12.44 over nearly 50 years.[3] Even in the 2020–21 season, an FA Cup Final ticket should cost me less than £15, not £45 and certainly not £115.[4] (And the price of a pre-match London pint in 1971 would be just as affordable at £1.40[5] in today's prices, not the £4.57[6] that it actually is.)

In 2017 I wasn't the only one thinking football fans were being priced out of the sport. During the Champions League game between Arsenal and Bayern Munich in March of that season, the visiting German fans staged a well-organised protest at the £80 ticket prices they were paying to watch the match.[7] Bayern's fans unfurled a banner which read 'Without Fans Football Is Not Worth A Penny' before throwing toilet rolls onto the pitch, causing the referee to hold up play while they were removed. Arsenal fans all pointedly applauded.

Money doesn't just make the world go round; it also gives us a universal index by which we can measure our economic and social standing in society. My salary tells me how I match up to my friends, colleagues and even members of my own family. It also provides me with a personal perspective on history. Because what I can afford to buy with my money today is also indicative of how well my generation is doing compared with those that came before.

We crave it, borrow it, work hard for it, steal it and perish when we don't have enough of it. There is always the hope that if we don't have money today we will get some tomorrow. And for many of us, it is this eternal hope which gives all our lives a sense of purpose, if perhaps not meaning.

But what happens when the social contract between the citizen and the economic system fails to produce enough winners? What happens when we can't get rich anymore? And how do we know when this is happening?

We all apply personal litmus tests to measure our economic well-being. Mine happens to be football. But I soon discovered that football is not the only entertainment that is out of kilter with the cost of modern living. In 2020 the average price of a cinema ticket was £7.50 (34p in 1971 and £1.88 in 1988) and a West End musical was £49.25 (£3.50 in 1971).[8] Some things have become cheaper, of course. Fifty years ago televisions were very expensive. If you wanted to watch television you rented one from somewhere like Radio Rentals or Rumbelows. These high-street electrical retailers also rented radios and hi-fi systems. If you had all three, then your home entertainment system was complete. A 1971 colour TV cost £289 (worth £3,700 in 2020) and a TV licence was £12 (£170.74). I was still renting my television from Currys in 1997. In the past 50 years, televisions have become so affordable (£98 for a 22-inch full HD LED from Amazon) that we own more tellies per household than ever before. Then again, we *require* so much more: an iPhone, tablet, laptop, broadband, subscriptions to Sky, Netflix, NOW TV, Spotify and Amazon Prime. An iPhone or a laptop is just as essential as a black-and-white telly was 50 years ago. Owning them is absolutely non-negotiable.

Much more sobering is the rising cost of property, which means millions of us have lost the chance of owning a home. The average house price in 1971 was £5,632. In May 2020 it had reached £235,673.[9] Taking proper account of inflation, the price of that same 1971 house today would be just £80,206.72. If salaries had risen as sharply as house prices, the average worker would be earning £90,000.[10] An average 1971 home cost four times typical annual earnings; today it is eight times.[11]

Everyone knows that house prices have sky-rocketed, but most people would still probably say that we're better off overall than we were 50 years ago. Just before the coronavirus struck, unemployment figures were at the lowest since the government started recording them in 1971. We enjoy unrestricted, easy access to credit and instead of mortgages being limited to just twice the size of our salaries as they were in 1971, today we can borrow four times as much as we earn. At the same time, household income rises have actually been keeping up with inflation. An average annual salary 50 years ago was £2,000. If the average worker's pay packet had kept track with inflation it would be £28,482.50,[12] which is not far off what it is today. In 1971, a century after the invention of the telephone, only half of British households had one. Now there are more phones than there are people. And the cost of a household staple like a supermarket chicken is much cheaper than it was in 1971. So what's the problem?

This long view of the link between inflation and earnings masks what has happened since the 2008 financial crisis, when wages started to fall behind inflation so that in real terms the average wage is worth less now than it was during the crash.[13] Overall economic growth has been very weak while productivity is at an all-time low. In fact, pay growth is at its weakest since the Napoleonic Wars.[14]

Look more closely at these record employment figures and you will find that millions of those new jobs are low paid and insecure. When the coronavirus started laying waste to the economy, people employed in these jobs were the first to be let go. In 1971 a job meant a reliable salary and protected working conditions. Today many of these new jobs are zero-hours contracts, freelance or low-hour part-time work. The rise in the number of people taking these kinds of jobs has given birth to a new phenomenon – 'in-work poverty' – such that eight million people currently living in poverty are part of a working family.[15] Britain's poorest families are still suffering from the shocks of the last recession and have responded by sending more family members out to work. In turn, businesses have taken advantage of this glut of low-paid employees.[16] Instead of a regular working week, we work when the phone buzzes or the boss calls. And workers aren't just competing against each other for jobs – they are fighting to match the production output of machines run by artificial intelligence.[17]

The number of hours we are working is no longer falling as it had been until the financial crash of 2008. According to the Resolution Foundation, those of us who are lucky enough to have salaries are working almost one hour per week more than they would have been if the post-1980s trend towards working fewer weekly hours had continued.[18] And more of us are working well past our middle years. People over age 50 now make up about a third of the entire UK work force, up from around one in five in the early 1990s. Living costs are rising fast and meagre pensions or limited savings are forcing us to stay in work longer.

There is further evidence that the UK is not experiencing the record low jobless levels which politicians so love to crow about. The Organisation for Economic Co-operation and Development (OECD) estimates the true figure is three times the official number because more than three million people who report themselves as 'economically inactive' to government labour force surveys are not included in the headline unemployment rate. By reinstating students, retirees and family carers, the OECD argues the national jobless figure should be increased from 4.6 percent to 13.2 percent of the working-age population not in education. Certainly in our northern cities the boast of high employment is not being borne out in the job centres. In Liverpool, according to the Centre for Cities, one in five people not in education can't find work. Of course the coronavirus crisis has worsened the economic situation for millions of families and pushed many more into poverty.

And long before the fateful spring of 2020, Britain's productivity levels already were in crisis, the worst since the start of the Industrial Revolution 250 years ago.[19] The 2019 figures from the ONS[20] show that after a period of steady growth throughout the 1990s and noughties, productivity has flatlined. In a worrying commentary, the ONS says that productivity since the economic downturn in 2008 has actually been 'growing more slowly than during the long period prior to downturn'. Productivity growth is important because more output per hour increases salaries and profits, improves standards of living and enables the tax-take to grow, which allows the government to fund better public services. Such a sustained period of minimal labour productivity growth has been called the UK's 'productivity puzzle' and is arguably the defining economic question of our age.

But the normal rules of domestic economics no longer seem to apply.[21]

The weak performance of Britain's economy since the financial crash would once have been consistent with an unemployment rate of 14 percent, not under 4 percent. In the 1970s a 4 percent jobless rate would have triggered shooting pay rises as employers competed for fewer workers. Instead, 70 percent of those in work in the UK are defined as 'chronically broke' – there's just too much month at the end of their money.[22] Millions of us in the UK are £100 away from a financial crisis, meaning that life could quickly be derailed by a dentist's appointment. Stella Creasy, the Labour MP for Walthamstow, east London, says: 'Every day has become a "rainy day", with a third of us having less than £500 in savings, so if the car breaks down or the washing machine goes on the blink, borrowing can be the only way to keep life moving'.

The struggle to keep a family fed and clothed is becoming more desperate as we find we have less to spend. In 2003 households on the lower half of incomes typically earned £14,900. In 2016–17 that figure had fallen to £14,800 (adjusted for inflation and housing costs).[23] Meanwhile, the Joseph Rowntree Foundation estimates that the benefits freeze has dragged 200,000 more people into poverty since 2016, around half of them children. More and more people than ever are being forced to turn to food banks. Between 1 April 2018 and 31 March 2019, the Trussell Trust, the biggest food bank distributor in the UK, handed out a record 1.6 million three-day emergency food supplies to people in crisis, a 19 percent increase on the previous year. More than half a million of these emergency food items went to children.[24] And as household debt continues to soar, millions of Brits now live in fear of a knock at the door from bailiffs.[25]

This is not a crisis confected by bleeding-heart socialists. In 2018 representatives from the United Nations, a body which aims to prevent citizens being abused by their nation states, spent 2 weeks in the UK investigating extreme poverty. After the visit, the head of the mission concluded that levels of child poverty in the UK were 'not just a disgrace, but a social calamity and an economic disaster'. Philip Alston, UN rapporteur on extreme poverty and human rights, said the UK government has inflicted 'great misery' on its people with 'punitive, mean-spirited and often callous' austerity policies driven by a political desire to carry out social engineering rather than economic necessity.

The government's response was to shoot the messenger. Rather than consider what was being said and take time to review the analysis, Amber Rudd, then in charge of the DWP, shot off a letter of official complaint to Mr Alston.[26] The mindset of politicians like Amber Rudd seems to be stuck in the economic equalities of 50 years ago when more people had the chance to get rich. In 1971 Britain was among the most equal countries on earth in terms of both household income and wealth. Today we are one of the most unequal.

At the top of the tree is a new super-elite group of money-making aristocrats, the 1 percent of highest-earning households in the world whose share of national income has ballooned in the past four decades from 3 percent in the late 1970s to about 8 percent today.[27] The top 1 percent of earners in the UK have almost doubled their share of total national income from 7 percent in 1981 to 17 percent in 2019.[28] A study on social mobility published by the Sutton Trust in 2020 found: 'There is no doubt that since the 1970s, the UK has seen the rise of income inequality in a form which would allow us to talk about elites pulling away economically, driven by a small number of occupations all based in finance'.[29]

Among these super-wealthy people the Institute for Fiscal Studies (IFS) has identified an elite within the elite – the 0.1 percent, 31,000 individuals in the UK, with incomes of a million pounds a year or more (living on 3,000, 5,000 or even £10,000 a day). For Danny Dorling, Oxford Professor and author of *Inequality and the 1%*, the telling moment came when the European Banking Authority released 'shocking' statistics showing that, after the banking crisis, the pay of UK bankers had begun to rise again so that in 2019 a record 3,567 were receiving more than €1 million a year, with the average yearly salary of those in this group being £1,700,000 (£4,660 a day).[30]

The gap between these big earners and ordinary workers is exemplified by the pay scales enjoyed by the chief executives of FTSE 100 companies. The average CEO earned the annual salary of his average employee within 3 working days of 2020.

(And the average CEO is almost always a he: in 2015 there were more executives and chairs of FTSE 100 companies named 'John' than there were women.)[31] In 2018 the average FTSE 100 CEO annual pay package was £3.46 million, equivalent to £901.30 an hour. In comparison, the average (as defined by the median) full-time worker took home £29,559 a year, equivalent to £14.37 an hour. Is the average boss really worth 117 times more than their average employee?[32] We think of Victorian society as being intolerably unequal, but in the late 1800s the governor of the Bank of England was paid just ten times more than a gentleman's butler.[33]

Household wealth in Britain today is even more unfairly distributed. In the 2 years between April 2016 and March 2018 our national wealth – including property, cash savings, shares and pensions – rose by 13 percent (after adjusting for inflation) to a record £14.6 trillion.[34] But the stockpile is spread wildly unevenly: the top 10 percent of households own almost half, while the wealth of the poorest fifth has declined in real terms. In the US, the Democracy Collaborative, a research and development institute, found that three people – Bill Gates, Jeff Bezos and Warren Buffett – had acquired a winning habit for accumulating wealth and now had more than the combined wealth of 160 million Americans. For many of the super-wealthy, being comfortably, or even extraordinarily, rich has never been enough.[35]

As far back as 1899 the American economist Thorstein Veblen coined the phrase 'conspicuous consumption' to describe the way rich people felt compelled to show everyone else they were rich. Victorian and Edwardian Britons who indulged in ostentatious displays of wealth tended to invest in extravagant houses, hire armies of servants or take a box at the opera. Today it is super-yachts and private jets, and rather than the opera, it is paying for hospitality suites at sporting events. In 1971 the entire seating at football grounds, apart from perhaps a few reserved seats in the directors' box, was taken up by working men on average salaries. Now, 46 percent of people earning net incomes over £200,000 say they watched live sport, compared with just 23 percent of those with incomes less than £46,000.[36]

While the super-rich are getting even richer, middle-class families, the backbone of Britain since the Industrial Revolution, are seeing their incomes stagnating as they are squeezed by their wealthier neighbours. The middle classes are being 'hollowed out', with decreasing chances of rising prosperity and growing fears of job insecurity. Instead of dreaming of getting rich, they are staving off debt as their salaries struggle to keep up with inflation. At the same time, even historically safe middle-class jobs, such as in insurance and law, are being threatened by artificial intelligence and automation. And although their houses are rising in value, they can't take advantage of the fact because they can't afford to move.[37]

Which brings us to perhaps the worst news of all: social mobility is rare, and it has become much harder to earn your way to high wealth. One in five men in professional occupations who were born between 1955 and 1961 became socially mobile, but the figure for those born between 1975 and 1981 is only one in eight.[38]

Fifty years ago someone with a good salary could save enough over the course of their working lives to retire with sufficient wealth to enjoy a financially secure retirement.[39] According to the Resolution Foundation a middle-income family of today relying on a single salary of £26,000 will have to save everything for 96 years to acquire the wealth of a household in the top 10 percent.[40] (In 2008 it would have taken just 60 years.) Under this law of diminishing returns even the highest-paid members of society can only hope to get really rich by winning the lottery or marrying into wealth.

In 2019 a Nobel Prize-winning economist agreed to head the most ambitious investigation yet into inequality in Britain. Sir Angus Deaton, with the support of the IFS, is spending 5 years not only tackling the gross disparities in wealth and income but also the plight of those toiling on a middle income. Sir Angus is concerned that inequality in Britain risks putting the country on the same path as the US to become one of the most unequal nations on earth.

He warns that democratic capitalism is only working for *part* of the population:

> You get an elite who think they did it all on their own and they deserve their position, and the people who didn't pass exams feel left behind. First they think the system is rigged, which is a reasonable thing to think, and then also partly blame themselves. We've created this [illusion of a] meritocratic aristocracy and people who didn't make it are pissed off.[41]

It is a point of view recognised by other economists. Martin Wolf, writing in the *Financial Times*, hardly a Marxist propaganda free sheet, warns: 'Over the past four decades, and especially in the US, the most important country of all, we have observed an unholy trinity of slowing productivity growth, soaring inequality and huge financial shocks'. The stark headline in the *Financial Times*, 'Why rigged capitalism is damaging liberal democracy', shocked many of its affluent readers in the City.[42]

But perhaps most astonishing of all were comments made by the Chancellor of the Exchequer, Philip Hammond, in 2019, when he was interviewed on *Newsnight*. He acknowledged that for many people, the market economy was not working as it was 'supposed to' and warned that the idea the economy is 'generating and distributing wealth is at odds with the practice that they are experiencing'.[43] Capitalism is no longer working because the City has for too long focused on short-term financial gain, which is being extracted from a work force making tangible contributions to the economy outside the financial markets. We know their true value now because these contributors are the same people the government termed key workers at the height of the coronavirus crisis. So it is hardly surprising that they are now asking themselves why they are not benefiting from a capitalist society if they *really* are so critical to it.

Well before the coronavirus plunged the world's economies into stagnation, trust in capitalism was ebbing. In January 2020, just as the global rich were gathering at the World Economic Forum in Davos, Switzerland, a survey was released which shattered global confidence in market capitalism. The Edelman 2020 Trust Barometer found that 56 percent of the population agreed that 'capitalism as it exists today does more harm than good in the world'.[44] Added to this, 65 percent said governments don't have a vision for the future that they can get behind.

In the run-up to Christmas 2019, Andrew Marr felt compelled to use his BBC flagship political programme to make an impassioned plea not to ignore the growing homelessness crisis in the UK. Citing Alston's UN report he said:

I'm not getting party political, but if we don't notice the rough sleepers all around us at this time of year, as the sleet comes down and the Christmas lights go up, then there is something wrong with all of us.

I don't know if this is more or less comforting, but it's probably not your fault. We can't help people worse off than ourselves if we are all battling our own financial struggles. It doesn't seem to matter how hard we work – we just can't get rich.

Across the Atlantic a Fox News anchor was coming to the same conclusions. In a 15-minute diatribe, Tucker Carlson denounced market capitalism, Wall Street exploitation, private equity, payday-loan outlets and America's ruling class. He later explained: 'A country where a shrinking percentage of the population is taking home an ever-expanding proportion of the money is not a recipe for a stable society'.[45]

What's happening in Britain and America is happening all over the world. Nearly half of all global pay is scooped up by only 10 percent of workers, according to the International Labour Organization, while the lowest-paid 50 percent receive only 6.4 percent. And the lowest-paid 20 percent – about 650 million workers – get less than 1 percent of total pay, a figure that has barely moved in 13 years.[46] A worker in the top 10 percent receives $7,445 a month (£5,866), while a worker in the bottom 10 percent gets only $22 (£17). The average pay of the bottom half of the world's workers is $198 (£150) a month.

The richest economies are now feeling the strain. In France, the *gilet jaunes* movement spawned protests over tax cuts for the wealthy and French society's growing inequality. In Britain, Brussels has been blamed for ending aspiration in communities which are cut adrift from a share of the nation's wealth. Sensing the growing discontent with government austerity policies, the 2019 election campaign was a staggering display of reckless multi-billion-pound spending promises by all the parties. Far from reassuring the public, it seemed to add insult to injury for ordinary people who every month have to manage their household budgets carefully.

Boris Johnson made it worse by pledging to cut taxes for the rich and the wealthy in a cynical betrayal of the scriptures written by the founding fathers of capitalism. Politicians have too easily forgotten that the godfather of capitalism, Adam Smith, warned of the dangers of extreme inequality back in 1759:

> A man of great fortune, a nobleman, is much farther removed from the condition of his servant than a farmer… The disproportion betwixt them, the condition of the nobleman and his servant, is so great that he will hardly look at him as being of the same kind; he thinks he has little title even to the ordinary enjoyments of life, and feels but little for his misfortunes.[47]

The lack of opportunity confronting Western populations suggests there is a structural failure in the traditional model for the creation and distribution of income and wealth. Millennials, middle classes and pensioners are all facing bleak economic futures. Many people have given up on getting rich and have settled for surviving in the short term. But even this modest goal is out of reach to those in society whom we rely on the most: the nurses, the policemen and women, the teachers, the firefighters and the carers. These first responders are the canaries in the dirty coal mine of capitalism. When the people who care for us and keep us alive can't afford to keep doing it, we should all start to feel worried.

1

WHAT IS RICH?

THE BILLIONAIRE WHO THINKS
EVERYBODY IS WORTH £660,791

By the time Warren Buffett, the world's most consistently rich individual, was sixteen, he had already saved $9,800, worth about $103,000 (£80,000) today. In 2019 his estimated wealth had mushroomed to $86 billion (£67 billion). He knows perhaps more than anyone that the business of getting rich requires a lifetime of industry.

In a speech in 1999 to the Nebraska Educational Forum, Buffett declared that we all have the potential to earn a minimum of $500,000 (£384,482) before we die. (That's £660,791 today.) When Buffett meets a young person starting out in life, he offers to buy 10 percent of their earning capacity. He'll pay you £66,000 now if you agree to give him everything you ever earn. It's an entertaining icebreaker. But what is curious about this figure is that it isn't very high. This is because Buffett has carefully calculated what people are really worth. In truth, if you worked for 40 years on an average income, you would have earned more than £1 million. Buffett didn't become the world's richest man without knowing when to undervalue a stock before making his bid.

In this country we use many economic indicators to evaluate the wealth and riches of our citizens. We are continually separating workers into winners and losers based on how much they earn and what they own. The government operates a variety of schemes to assess this, the most obvious being the tax system, which sets the level for the highest-earning members of society at over £150,000, attracting the highest tax rate of 45 percent on income. Mirroring the tax threshold for the highest earners, the BBC publishes the names of all employees with salaries of more than £150,000. If you are paid less than £150,000 in the BBC you are allowed to retain your anonymity.

In 2019 the Labour Party made its own determination of who was rich, setting a super-tax threshold for anyone earning more than £80,000, which it argued represented the top 5 percent of the population. The public sector also sets levels of earnings which bar rich people from qualifying for discounts, subsidies and social housing. Anyone earning less than £12,500 is exempt from paying income tax, while local authorities allow citizens to qualify for reduced-rent council accommodation if they earn less than £60,000. The Conservatives have suggested extending this council accommodation benefit to those earning as much as £100,000.[1] That's not far off the joint income of £120,000 that some private schools set as the highest threshold for a family claiming a bursary for the education of their children.

The government also casts a value judgement on the assets of individual citizens. If you have assets worth more than £325,000 you are considered sufficiently wealthy to be compelled to pay inheritance tax, while anyone with savings of more than £16,000 is denied the right to claim Universal

Credit. And a sliding scale of deductions is taken from any benefit claimants who have more than £6,000 but less than £16,000 in savings.

But in this chapter we are much more interested in the rich than the poor. I want to find a golden figure which tells us what we need to earn before we can unquestionably and definitively describe ourselves as rich.

The Institute for Fiscal Studies[2] (IFS) has helpfully identified a group of 310,000 individuals who make up the very top 1 percent of income tax payers in the UK. To qualify, you require a taxable income of at least £160,000. This figure is lowered to £120,000 after the IFS includes the 43 percent of British adults who don't pay any income tax. Those already in the top 1 percent might look up enviously at the top 0.5 percent and 0.1 percent of income tax payers, who respectively earn £236,000 and £650,000 in taxable income each year.

The top 1 percent of income tax payers are disproportionately male, middle-aged and based in London. A man aged 45–54 in London could be in the top 1 percent nationally while still needing a further £550,000 to be in the top 1 percent for his gender, age and region. Those born in the baby-boomer generation, who have benefited from rising house prices and generous final salary pensions, are disproportionately richer. And such patterns become more pronounced at even higher income levels. Almost half of the top 0.1 percent of income tax payers are based in London, over 40 percent are aged 45–54 and only 11 percent are women.[3] The Resolution Foundation has calculated that to break into the top 10 percent of families by wealth, your savings, shares and income have to be higher than £670,000 per adult member of the family. Wealth of

£105,000 per adult would put you in the top half of the population. By contrast, debt and a lack of property and pension wealth means the bottom 10 percent of families have less than £3 in wealth per adult.[4]

The Organisation for Economic Co-operation and Development (OECD), tasked with improving economic performance across the world, has calculated that the middle-class financial threshold for a two-person household living in the UK registers at between £1,711 and £4,561 per month after tax. Using the OECD figures a couple earning more than £79,648.55 can safely describe themselves as rich.[5,6] This is lower than the UK government's own figure of £94,200 before tax for the median income of a couple in the top tenth decile of UK earners.[7]

The levels of wealth required by foreigners who come to Britain are set higher than for those of our own citizens. Under the golden visa scheme for wealthy immigrants the Home Office will offer a right of residence if the applicant has £2 million to invest in the UK. This grants very rich investors the right to settle in the UK after 5 years. Should they have £10 million in earnings and investments, they are allowed to shorten the process and apply to reside here after just 2 years.[8] At the lower end, you may be turned away if you don't earn enough money. The Centre for Social Justice, co-founded by former Tory leader Iain Duncan Smith MP, has urged the government to set the minimum salary for immigrant workers coming to the UK after Brexit at £37,700. That is £7,000 more than the average British wage and £13,000 more than the starting salary of a nurse. Under these rules immigrant workers who don't meet this means test will be excluded from Britain.

Accumulating riches is an organic and often transient endeavour. We need time to make our money and when we do we may not have it for long. The top 1 percent of income tax payers are not a fixed group – a quarter of those in the top 1 percent in 1 year will not be there the next. After 5 years only half will still be in the top 1 percent. As a result, someone has a much higher chance of being in the top 1 percent at some point in their lives than they do in any given year. Furthermore, 3.4 percent of all people (and 5.5 percent of men) born in 1963 were in the top 1 percent of income tax payers at some point between 2000 and 2016.[9]

We live in a neo-liberal capitalist society that makes us compete against one another for our wealth and worth. So it is understandable we should want to know how well we are performing compared with work colleagues, neighbours and family. Culturally we do this by comparing annual salaries, although of course the British are rather shy about sharing this very personal information and opening ourselves up to judgement. But we do know that in the UK in 2019, the median annual salary was £30,420 (£585 a week and £24,220 a year after tax and National Insurance) according to the Office for National Statistics.[10]

However, valuing ourselves around the median annual salary isn't all that informative. The statisticians at the IFS have developed an online calculator, which gives us a much more nuanced view. Rather than just using a crude salary, their algorithm takes account of the size of the family and includes all the income contributed by all the household adults, while also making deductions for income taxes, National Insurance and council tax. Using the median full-time salary of £30,420,[11] and allowing for two adults and two children under thirteen with a council tax of £1,000, the IFS result reads: 'You have a higher income than around 35 percent of the population – equivalent to about 22.5 million individuals'.[12]

But we want more. Our high salary suddenly doesn't seem quite so important if our friends somehow still manage to live in a bigger house, take more holidays or drive a very expensive car. Perhaps a better test of an individual's riches is *disposable* income. According to the ONS, in 2018 households in the bottom 20 percent of the population had on average an annual 'equivalised'[13] disposable income of £12,798, while the top 20 percent had £69,126.[14]

We are in a constant state of material progression from a fixed starting point to a golden retirement, with markers highlighting our financial and material achievements along the way. Those in their sixties – the baby-boomers – are the wealthiest age group, with average wealth equivalent to £332,000. Many are at the end of a career and have had time to accumulate savings, pensions and property. By contrast, those in their eighties have £186,000 in wealth, while individuals in their thirties have £55,000. Twenty-somethings, who may be on the first rung of the career ladder with no accumulated earnings behind them, have just £2,000.[15] Accordingly, Thomas Stanley and William Danko, authors of a 1990s study on the nature of wealth, *The Millionaire Next Door*, have devised an elegant formula for working out your average net worth based on age: multiply your age by your pre-tax income, and divide by ten. So if you are 30 years old and earn the median salary of £30,420, your individual score is 91,260. And you can measure that against others, not just of your age but further on in their careers.

We may make a ballpark assessment of how well someone is doing by their career choice, but looks can be misleading. True, a top Queen's Counsel can earn in excess of £2 million a year, whereas the highest-earning bricklayer will reach peak earnings at £90,000.[16] But it is perhaps reassuring to know that the median earnings for a barrister are £60,000[17] while the median bricklayer's pay packet amounts to £42,000.

It's also worth looking at things from another perspective entirely: the 'Giving What We Can' evaluator is part of the Centre for Effective Altruism and is the brainchild of Toby Ord, an Australian moral philosopher. By entering your net income – say our £30,420 median salary for a family of four – our apparently bog-standard earnings instantly look pretty rosy, putting us among the 16.3 percent richest of the global population.[18]

Does this comfort us or contextualise our privilege in a meaningful way? Does it identify who is *really* rich in Britain today?

I have taken a basket of estimates from the government and the private sector (largely discussed above), which all convey benefits or penalties for the highest earners and then found an average (mean) figure for the UK. Gathering all these different perspectives together, we can say that if you as an individual earn a salary of more than £103,427.62, you can call yourself rich.[19]

Now let's find out why so few of us will ever achieve it.

2

SURVIVORS

THE INSURANCE SALESMAN WHO DIDN'T LEAVE HIS HOME FOR 4 YEARS

I first met David in a waiting room of an advice charity where he was chatting up a pregnant, homeless Bulgarian woman.

As I greeted him in the doorway he enthusiastically informed me, 'I told her I liked her and I asked her on a date, but I don't think she wants to go'.

I looked across at the woman, now obliviously tapping away on her phone, worried that he might have been harassing her.

David is 63 years old, has long, lank grey hair and struggles with his weight. His rambling attempt at a chat-up didn't even register with her. Her own problems had silenced most of life's peripheral noises. She was at least 6 months pregnant, with two other kids at home being looked after by her out-of-work brother. She had run out of money. Her commitments to her children meant she couldn't work and now Brexit was threatening to return her to Bulgaria where she feared her abusive husband would soon find her.

David hadn't *really* noticed her either. He suffers from bipolar disorder, and this was one of his up days. It is a feature of his condition that he speaks to everyone he comes into contact with when he feels well enough to go out. He's all over them with propositions and promises which he can't possibly deliver. On bad days he doesn't leave his flat.

There was a period in his life when his illness was so bad he hadn't been able to leave his flat for 4 years. He just couldn't summon the mental strength to engage with the world. He was fortunate that his sister brought him food and tidied up every now and then. She also dealt with some of his more pressing correspondence. But for 4 years he had almost no human contact.

David wasn't always so ill-equipped for life. He once enjoyed a good job in the City selling building insurance to restaurants. He could afford to take out a mortgage on a modest two-bed house in Woking, well inside Surrey's affluent commuter belt. Shortly afterwards he met a girl, Wendy, on his train to work, and the two began a long-term relationship. She moved in with him. In those days David's future was pretty bright.

But then the recession hit – not the last one, but the one in the early 1990s when the rapid increase in house prices resulted in an overheated housing market – and David's home was plunged into negative equity. The property slump followed the late 1980s housing boom which had in turn been driven by steep interest rate cuts to maintain the pound's competitiveness against the deutschmark. It was a recipe for financial disaster. The interest rate cut set off high inflation.[1]

By 1989 the base rate had jumped from 7.5 to 15 percent, transforming once-affordable mortgages into financial mill-stones around hundreds of thousands of first-time buyers' necks. But the final screw was turned when the John Major government decided to join the European Exchange Rate

Mechanism (ERM), effectively locking Britain into Germany's high interest rates. The City could smell a profit. Over the previous months speculators like George Soros, an extraordinarily wealthy hedge fund manager, had been building a huge 'short' position in sterling that would become immensely profitable if the pound fell below the lower band of the ERM. A 'short' is an invidious investment strategy because you can only profit if a business, industry or currency fails. Soros and the other hedge fund speculators had sold sterling at its high water mark with an option to buy it back when it fell. They rightly judged that the linkage between the two economies looked highly vulnerable – although not as vulnerable as when the financiers made their move.[2]

They gambled that the Treasury would be unable to keep sterling at the high rates of exchange that it was now locked into. As the British economy struggled to match Germany's, the UK government tried to prop up the depreciating pound. John Major's Chancellor, Norman Lamont, raised interest rates to 10 percent and authorised the spending of billions in foreign currency reserves to buy up the sterling being sold on the currency markets. For a short while this prevented the pound falling below its minimum level in the ERM.

Then the money men made their move.

On Tuesday, 15 September 1992, Soros' Quantum Fund began a massive sell-off of sterling – $10 billion's worth. George Soros led a field of speculators who, after borrowing UK gilts, started selling them and then buying them back later at even cheaper prices. They repeated the trick every few minutes, making a profit every time.[3]

The more the UK government fought back by propping up the pound, the more the speculators stood to gain. Britain finally hoisted the white flag on 16 September 1992, when the government was forced to withdraw sterling from the ERM. That day has gone down in economic history as Black Wednesday and it cost the UK Treasury £3.4 billion. The speculators, meanwhile, won personal fortunes. Soros alone made over £1 billion in profit by short selling sterling, winning the epithet 'the man who broke the Bank of England'.

All economic breakdowns have echoes in past financial crashes. Soros can be compared to Jesse Livermore, an American stock trader who shorted the markets in the crash of 1929 and walked away with $1.4 billion in today's money. Soros parlayed his 1992 gains into a net worth of $23 billion. In hindsight, the gamble looked like a no-brainer. Sixteen years later the same gamblers shorted the 2008 housing markets, turning 1992's millionaires into billionaires and making Soros even more money.[4]

But Britain's calamitous withdrawal from the ERM in 1992 didn't only have an impact on property prices. Record numbers of businesses up and down the country failed.[5] Among them was David's employer, a small insurance business in the City specialising in selling or 'brokering' business insurance for Indian restaurants. These 'tandoori-boom' restaurants, which had rapidly expanded by buying up overpriced prime real estate in London, were particularly vulnerable to falling property prices and high interest rates. When they started to tumble, the knock-on effect left David's company badly exposed. Hit by huge claims from the restaurants and a vanishing business model, the owners started laying people off.

David discovered he was to be one of the first out of the door when he noticed a curiously handwritten letter in his pigeonhole at work addressed to his home in Woking. The chief executive officer apologised for not being able to speak to David personally but the recession had hit the company hard and there was no time for personal formalities. David left the office the same day and spent the journey back to Woking, still tightly clutching the letter, staring disbelievingly out of the train window.

'It was a real kick in the teeth as I thought I was pretty good at my job', he later recalled. 'I hit my targets regularly, got along with the Indian restaurant owners and I could always turn a lead into a sale. I loved my free curries'.

David was one of 3 million people to lose their jobs in 1992. He remained confident he would get another one and in the coming days applied to dozens of insurance companies. But the City was in the grip of a virulent recession and there weren't enough jobs to go around. Wendy tried to help him out but she was feeling insecure in her own job, an assistant sales director at a leading industrial paint company. 1992 was not the year to start repainting buildings.

David reckoned, perhaps rightly, that he couldn't afford to lose touch with his contacts in the City. The insurance markets of the late 1980s and early 1990s were as much oiled by liquid lunches as they were by high premiums, and it was all about who you knew. He blew all of his redundancy pay-off buying lunches and paying for nights out with his 'old pals'. When that started to run out, David fell back on his credit cards. With no job in sight and his credit cards maxed out, Wendy left him.

Losing his job and his girlfriend in the space of a few weeks left David feeling helpless. It wasn't long before the mortgage company foreclosed, forcing him to give up his house in the suburbs. But that still left him with a negative equity debt of nearly £50,000. David had little choice but to move in with his ageing parents who lived even further away from the city. David suffered a mental breakdown and fell into deep depression.

The once ebullient insurance salesman shut himself away from the outside world for 4 years, building debt all the while. He signed anything to make the debt collectors go away. He now owed at least four credit card companies a total of £67,000.

He is one of tens of thousands of forgotten casualties from a recession few people even remember today. Because their stories are one recession removed from the headlines, most people can't relate to them. They are living unnoticed among our communities, coping as best they can, heavily dependent on benefits and too old to work.

When I met him, David was agitated and very talkative, rattling off concerns and complaints about the people who featured in the daily struggles of his life: the council housing officer, the electricity company, the debt collection agency, even members of his family. But he retains a disarming sense of self-awareness and insight about what has happened to him. His poverty and crippling illness may have left him destitute, reliant on the grace of the state for survival, but when he's well enough to venture out, he is as charming company as you are likely to meet. His poverty has not left him without dignity though the quality of his life is deeply compromised. He told me:

> I know I won't work again, not in a job that means anything to me or tests my intellect. I also know that I will probably never have sex again. I won't ever experience the feeling of a soft human body rubbing against mine.

It was a strange but very honest assessment of both his employment and romantic prospects. My encounter with David was one of the many conversations I have had with people who have lost everything but retain a forceful independent human spirit that cut me to the quick. Poverty doesn't just remove people from the world of work and the material comforts one associates with a regular salary. It chips away at the qualities that make life worth living and makes us question what versions of life are *worth* living.

In the early stages of the 2008–09 recession, it looked like it would be very different from the last. It had started in the City and it was the banks who were shedding all the jobs. I remember being in Canary Wharf, where I was working as a reporter for the *Independent* newspaper, watching all the young shell-shocked bankers milling outside Lehman Brothers clasping cardboard boxes that contained all their personal possessions. This time it was going to be a 'white-collar' recession, unlike anything seen in the past. The rest of us appeared to be bystanders while the City bonuses went up in smoke. But that's not how it turned out, because that's not how *any* of these recessions turn out.

In the end it is the low-skilled workers, those at the bottom of the pile – the shelf-stackers and cleaners, the plant and machine operatives – who have suffered most since 2008. Those working in the trades, the plumbers and the motor mechanics, have caught only a dose of unemployment. Eleven years after the financial crisis, then the deepest recession since the Second World War, workers' real pay packets were smaller than in 2007. And according to pre-pandemic forecasts by the Office for Budget Responsibility, it was not to return to the 2007 level until 2023. To put it another way, even before the economic shock of the coronavirus, it was going to take us 15 years just to get back to where we started. For those who have clung to employment, many have found themselves even more at risk of losing their job.[6]

Eleven years after the recession, research showed that low-income households in Britain were more vulnerable to another economic slowdown than they were before the financial crisis. The Resolution Foundation found that a decade of weak wage growth left the poorest UK households and middle-income families less prepared for another downturn. It also warned that the gradual dismantling of the benefits system under the policy of austerity imposed over the past decade by Conservative-led governments has left people without the same degree of support. Contrast this with the news in 2019 that bankers' pay was on the rise again.

The Institute for Social and Economic Research conducted a study of unemployment after the early 1990s recession (which halted David's life). It identified longer-term consequences for workers losing their jobs now. It also found that the experience of unemployment can damage people's chances of keeping a job once they find one again. And the living standards of families more dependent on wages and salaries – such as working-age adults without children and couples with children – are more affected by recessions than people on state benefits, such as pensioners and lone parents.

The rules of inequality during a recession are not straightforward. Inequality fell during the recession of the mid-1970s, rose during that of the early 1980s and was more or less unchanged during the early 1990s recession. But in all these recessions, incomes in the middle of the income distribution

– those on the verge of getting rich – fell more than those at the bottom.[7] Sadly, you have to be on a middle income to have something to lose. By not learning the lessons of the past two recessions we are wading heavily through a third, this time compounded by a pandemic that has wreaked havoc on already impoverished households and a weakened economy.

3

FIRST RESPONDERS

THE HUNGRY NURSE WHO ATE
THE PATIENT'S SANDWICH

Sally Potter wanted to be a nurse ever since she was a young girl growing up in Newport, Shropshire. In 2008 she left school and started an adult nursing degree at a university in London. Four years later her parents and friends cheered and clapped when she was presented with her nursing certificate at the hospital's graduation ceremony. But qualification had come at a price: in realising her ambition Sally had incurred debts of more than £8,000. Although she was lucky enough to graduate under the nursing bursary scheme, which paid for her tuition, it barely scratched the surface of her daily living expenses:

> I didn't have a typical student life of nightclubs and partying – I got my head down and got on with the studying and the placement work. But I couldn't make the bursary stretch a full term, and for the last 3 weeks of nearly every term I had to borrow money from my mum and friends.

Sally reckoned that as soon as she got her first real nursing job she would claw back her debts and start living within her means.

But it didn't turn out like that.

Her starting salary as a full-time nurse was £21,000, which worked out at an hourly rate of £10.10, then 45p less than the London living wage. Her employers took £265.33 of her wages each month to pay directly to HMRC, leaving her with an annual net wage of £17,816. So Sally began each month with £1,484.66 in her pocket. Out of this she had to pay her monthly £700 rent for a room in a sub-let council flat in east London. Her share of the heating and electricity bill was £85 a month. But if she was careful, and didn't eat out, she could keep the groceries and household essentials down to £65 a week. Travel to and from the hospital using two buses was capped at £21.10 a week. As a student nurse she had been exempt from council tax, but now she had to pay £1,000 a year for her local services. This left her with £272.26 each month or £68.06 each week. But because Sally still had to pay back £30 a week for her £8,000 student nursing loan, she ended up with just £38.06 a week for extras and budgeting emergencies like a lost or broken mobile phone.

Her treats budget, held over for alcohol on special occasions, was used up on new clothes and her emergency savings were wiped out on a trip to Shropshire to visit her sister in hospital following a car crash. Sally was soon struggling to make ends meet. The crunch time came 3 weeks into winter when the heating bills began to rise. She got locked out of the flat while her flatmate was away and had to pay a locksmith to let her back in. It was an unexpected bill she couldn't afford to pay:

By the end of the month I hoped that my next pay cheque cleared before I started to worry about where my next meal was coming from. I tried to save by getting up early and walking to work so I didn't have to pay for the bus. But I soon found out that it was costing me as much in food to give me energy for the extra walking as it would have done if I had caught the bus and cut out breakfast.

Sally's health began to suffer, she felt listless and run down, and so she took a Friday and Monday off to give her body a chance to recover. As a result she was docked 2 days of pay. 'I was 5 days short of 6 months of employment, so I did not qualify for sick pay', she complained at the time:

Unfortunately, that month I needed to pay the Nursing and Midwifery Council (NMC) registration fee. On calling the NMC to discuss the situation, I asked if I could set up the instalment plan they had offered. I was told 'no', it's too late, even though it was 5 days prior to my deadline. I was told I needed to apply to set up direct debits in April as there was a 6-week set-up period. I suggested paying £30 today and setting up a direct debit to take the following instalments from September. But I was told I couldn't, I need to pay the full £120. 'You can set it up for next year!' she suggested, which wasn't helpful, as the problem was here and now, I told her. 'Can't you borrow some money to pay it?' she asked even more unhelpfully, and then added, 'If you don't pay it, you won't be able to work past your renewal date and will need to reapply to go on the register'.

Apparently, I am stupid as well as skint. The point to this is, I expected a little help and compassion in a time of need from those who regulate a profession based on care and compassion, and the outcome was surprisingly uncompassionate and uncaring.

Sally started borrowing from friends and family just so she could stay at work. But it was never enough and she soon found herself in a desperate situation:

This patient came on to the ward. She was about sixty and was being treated for varicose veins. She was in one of the holding cubicles, sitting on a chair waiting for some tests to come back. On the chair next to her was a half-eaten sandwich from the M&S in the hospital. I hadn't eaten all day. I'd been on shift since 7am caring for 9 patients while there was an outbreak of diarrhoea and vomiting affecting half the ward and someone else dying in the side room. I was exhausted and hungry, and I simply couldn't think how I was going to eat so I just went up to the patient and asked her if she was going to finish the sandwich. She looked shocked and embarrassed and just said 'take it' which she repeated several times. I grabbed it and wolfed it down in front of her and walked out of the cubicle without saying a word. Of course I was embarrassed but I just didn't care.

People sometimes question the claim that nurses really use food banks. They accuse nursing unions of scaremongering or exaggerating the problem. There have even been suggestions that one reason more nurses are using food banks is because the charities are offering more of them and so they are actually feeding a demand that isn't really there.

This is what wealthy investment banker David Freud told the House of Lords in 2013: 'If you put more food banks in, that is the supply. Clearly, food from the food banks is a free good and by definition with a free good there's almost infinite demand'.[1] Former Tory minister Edwina Currie went further and claimed that food banks make people poorer: 'Free food subsidises low wages; it helps support the black economy… It pauperises those it seeks to help. Like giving money to "homeless" beggars on London streets, it encourages more of what it seeks to relieve'.

More recently, in 2017, Dominic Raab, a Conservative Foreign Secretary and Boris Johnson stand-in, sparked fury by saying most food bank users are not 'languishing in poverty'. He went on to claim that 'the typical user…is someone who has a cash flow problem'.[2] This is, of course, palpable nonsense. The Royal College of Nursing (RCN), through its network of reps and RCN officers across the UK, has reported 'growing numbers of nursing staff using food banks, taking on additional jobs and accruing personal debt… This is not just one or two cases'. The Trussell Trust, the largest food bank network in the UK, confirmed it had had reports from [its] food banks of 'nurses being referred for emergency food'.

But nurses using food banks is really the tip of the iceberg. The RCN Foundation awarded over 500 financial hardship grants to working, retired, trainee or unemployed nurses, midwives and healthcare assistants in the UK in 2016. Two years later a record number of hardship grants worth £247,000 were awarded.

One in four grants for cost-of-living expenses went to a full-time nurse.[3] A further 6,500 trainee nurses have been awarded hardship grants from their universities since 2017.[4]

Cases like Sally's are real, and there are going to be more of them. In 2017 the government scrapped the bursary scheme, saddling thousands of nurses with new debt. The Royal College of Midwives predicts a fifth of all student midwives will graduate with debts of more than £10,000.[5] And the future for employed nurses is no brighter: the number of nurses using payday loans to get by rose to 35,000 in 2015, double the figure of 3 years earlier. Researchers estimate that this number has continued to grow.[6]

The government may wish to dismiss this as scaremongering but payday-loan companies are taking it very seriously. They know that poor nurses make excellent customers and have invested tens of thousands of pounds targeting them with adverts offering quick and easy loans at extortionate rates of interest. In October 2016 Western Circle, a 'technology & data oriented lending company' which owns the payday-loan company Cashfloat, published research based on a survey of 160,000 clients, claiming that 1 in 10 NHS nurses were then heavily dependent on payday loans.[7] In these stricken circumstances, it is hardly surprising so many nurses give up on the NHS. Indeed, two out of three nurses were thinking of leaving the NHS in 2020.[8] Nurses are already prepared for a difficult job caring for some of the most vulnerable people in our society, and it doesn't seem too much to ask that they might be able to afford to pay their electricity bill, buy the odd drink or item of clothing, maybe even take an occasional holiday. As it is, they are being forced to beg for food. The coronavirus has only exacerbated the situation, and in July 2020 requests for financial help were so great that the RCN Foundation had to close its COVID-19 Support Fund 'due to unprecedented demand'.[9]

Nurses are not the only workers among our emergency services struggling to get by. There have been cases of police officers in Brighton, on the south coast, joining nurses in the queue for the food bank. In 2017 Sussex Police Federation revealed that two of its officers had been forced to turn to food banks, while many more have been given food vouchers.[10] Federation chairman Matt Webb said his organisation has had to help numerous officers whose wages were unable to stretch to putting food on the family table.

Police constable starting salaries in Sussex are around £20,000 but, with the high cost of living in the area, this does not go very far. In 2017 the average rent for a one-bedroom property in Brighton was £957 per calendar month, leaving officers £463 to cover other household bills, food and fuel costs. For an officer thinking of starting a family, the cost of living very soon starts to look unworkable. A two-bed rented property is £1,365 per month, giving the average officer just £42 left over if they have to cover the whole rent themselves. I've spoken to one 40-year-old officer who is on £45,000 and has been forced to move back into his parents' council home.

This picture of vital work rewarded by marginal pay is reflected across all our emergency services – the people we expect so much from whenever we encounter a personal crisis in our own lives. For firefighters it must be particularly galling that although they often team up with local charities across the country to deliver food parcels to needy and isolated families, they can't adequately provide for themselves. After knocking off their shift, the same firefighters who have dropped off vital provisions for desperate members of the community go in search of food banks to feed their own families. The overwhelming sense of embarrassment and gratitude felt by public servants who avail themselves of food banks means they often end up paying back the charity by volunteering at the distribution centres outside of their already demanding working hours.[11]

Research shows that some emergency service employees are also struggling to pay their energy bills, with 81 percent having to ration central heating and electrical fan and oil heaters. Almost one in five emergency services personnel is in debt to their energy suppliers. The police have the greatest proportion in the red, followed by fire-service staff and nurses. In an effort to cut costs, hospital nurses, police officers, ambulance workers and firefighters have resorted to piling on warm clothes indoors rather than turning up the thermostat.[12] Perhaps saddest of all are the reports of hospital nurses working extra shifts partly to avoid going back to their cold homes.[13]

People whom we rely on as society's safety net – the nurses, the police and the firefighters – have always earned enough to live near the places where they are needed the most. They have never earned a lot, but they have always lived in the heart of the community. Not anymore. A combination of low wages and high rents and high utility bills have forced first responders out of the cities where they work. Today they are being priced out of their local communities by luxury developments, gentrification and raging property inflation. Mortgage lender Halifax found that on average a key worker can no longer afford to buy a home in 92 percent of towns in Britain.[14] There have even been cases of paramedics and nurses bedding down in local churches because they don't have enough salary to pay London's private rents.[15]

Of course this is a problem that was supposed to have been mitigated by a national building programme of priority key-worker accommodation. It was a nice idea. But time after time, public bodies have sold off to the highest bidder land which could be used for this purpose. Or large private developers, who have made solemn promises about the provision of affordable accommodation for key workers, have reneged by downgrading the offer once they have won planning permission.

The dearth of reasonably priced accommodation in the capital means more and more emergency service workers are having to commute into London. Ambulanceman Anthony Scantlebury says that this can take its toll on the efficiency of a typical worker:

> If you finish at 7pm in the evening, before you get home and get yourself sorted out, it is probably 10 o'clock at night. And then you need to leave home at half past four in the morning again to start work at seven… That cuts down on your sleep time and you get progressively more tired as the week goes on.[16]

A recent report on London firefighters revealed that 8 firefighters actually lived abroad, 26 more lived in Wales, 3 had chosen to move to Northern Ireland and 2 to Scotland. Other London firefighters were commuting in from as far as Truro, York and Darlington, 250 miles from the capital. More broadly, only 2,052 firefighters are able to afford to live in inner London and 1,049 in outer London, leaving 2,700 to get to work from locations across the 'rest of England'.[17] Such dispersal means firefighters are less familiar with the daily fire risks associated with their local neighbourhoods.

The encroachment of high-priced housing has also taken a toll on fire stations themselves. Between 2010 and 2018, 45 stations across the country were forced to close. And so, at the time of the Grenfell fire, in which 73 people lost their lives, very few of the London crews who attended the fire came from the local area. Fifty years ago every fire officer who manned the pumps in north Kensington, where Grenfell Tower is located, lived and worked in the locality. They were paid enough to cover the local rent and their bills and still had money left over to bring up a family in the community. There was an attainable and realistic career ladder, which meant if you started at the bottom you could climb up the pay scale, start a family and look forward to your retirement.

Since the 1980s pay scales have been flattening out such that a once common aspiration like working and living in the community where you were born has become harder and harder to realise. In September 2010 the starting salary for a new police constable was £23,300 in England and Wales. Eight years later constables were earning £23,100 (£200 less).[18] Taking into account inflation between 2010 and 2018 this amounts to a real-term reduction in pay of 16 percent (£4,300). And not all new constables will start on £23,100. The exact figure depends on skills and experience, but those with 'no qualifications' can expect a minimum salary of just under £20,000.[19]

Similar pay cuts have been imposed on nurses. When nurses qualify they start on Band 5 of the NHS pay scale. In April 2010 newly qualified nurses in England got paid a starting salary of about £21,200.[20] In 2018 new nurses started on £23,000.[21] Adjusting for inflation, new starter nurses are actually earning around £1,900 less than they would have in 2010. That's an 8 percent reduction in pay over 8 years.[22]

The change has been felt across the public sector. An inspirational teacher can transform a child's life chances. It is a profession to which the state used to attach great value. But while parents, who entrust teachers with more than 10 years of their children's life, recognise this contribution, successive chancellors appear to have been less bothered.

In 2010 the starting salary for teachers in England and Wales outside of London was £21,600.[23] In September 2017 a newly qualified teacher's minimum salary reached just £22,900.[24] Although this looks like a modest increase, taking into account inflation, it's actually a reduction of around £2,500 or 10 percent. And what about those public sector workers whose jobs are less glamorous but no less vital? Take the binmen of Merseyside: they may have been retitled 'recycling officers' but they still start on parlous salaries of just £14,363.[25] In 2010 binmen in the Midlands were starting on salaries of £17,800 and drivers were getting £21,500.[26]

The truth is that while previous generations took pay increases for granted, today public sector workers have seen their wages fall in real terms. In 2018 the Police Federation of England and Wales (PFEW) recorded three-quarters of its rank and file reporting feeling more financially worse off than they did in 2013 – not surprising since they lost 18 percent of their salary in real terms.[27] Half (44.8 percent) of those polled said they worried about the state of their personal finances either 'every day or almost every day'. More than one in nine (11.8 percent) said they either never or almost never had enough money to cover all of their essentials, while 3.8 percent had taken out a payday loan at least once in the past year.

As a result 10,000 police officers had asked permission to take on a second job. This was an increase from the year before, climbing from 6.3 to 7.8 percent countrywide. These second jobs included taxi driving, security work, gardening, plumbing and beauty therapy.

At the time John Apter, chair of the PFEW, said:

Our members are clearly suffering from even worse financial pressures than last year, with some appearing to be in dire straits. Our members are under immense pressure to deliver, with dwindling resources and rising crime – particularly violent crime – leading to a demand for our services that has never been higher. All they want is to be adequately paid for the job that they do.

He reminded the government:

We know officers are struggling and some have had to resort to food vouchers and other welfare schemes. This clearly cannot be right or acceptable that those employed to keep the public safe cannot make ends meet or put food on tables for their families.[28]

In the past, the government was always able to recruit highly motivated and conscientious members of the public with the promise of a generous pension in compensation for modest pay. Ever since Robert Peel's first 'Peelers' began patrolling London streets in 1829, a police officer knew that faithful service would be rewarded with a good pension. Under the final salary pension schemes of the 1990s and early noughties, some senior officers were retiring in their early fifties on pensions in excess of £100,000. Even mid-ranking officers could look forward to lives supported by pensions worth £60,000 with top-ups. The cream of Britain's crime fighters were literally getting rich by hanging up their helmets. But the future doesn't look quite so rosy now. In 2015 the government brought in laws that ended the generous final-salary schemes for public sector workers, including police officers. These golden-plated pensions were unsustainable for an ageing population which risked bankrupting pension funds and denying younger workers a financially secure retirement. Now a final pension would be based on the average pay an officer received during his or her entire career. Overnight, the police pension was halved. Instead of looking forward to a well-paid retirement after 30 years of public service, police officers today worry whether they will be able to support themselves into their old age. The same pensions changes have affected the long-term futures of firefighters, nurses and teachers.

Putting our sympathy to one side, there are serious consequences for wider society. A nurse who is preoccupied about feeding her own children or even herself can't be carrying out her job to the very best of her ability. What if Sally finds herself so hungry that she is not able to concentrate on the dozens of people whose lives are in her hands? A London fireman who has to drive 100 miles back to his family in Southend after his shift will have no idea about the local fire alarm drills at the schools where he used to send his children. And perhaps a police officer who is worried about repaying a payday loan might find themselves sorely tempted to take a backhander from a drug dealer who wants to get the local police off his back.[29]

No one ever expected to get rich by becoming a fire officer or a nurse, but it is a national disgrace that our first responders are commuting across the country, taking second jobs as taxi drivers, living off hardship grants and eating out of food banks. How strange that governments fall over themselves to pay respect to members of our emergency services in the New Year's Honours list or exhorted us to clap for these key workers every Thursday during the height of the pandemic, but they won't pay them enough to live on.

4

STRUGGLERS

THE BOY WHO MISSED HIS MOTHER'S FUNERAL

Darren Reid's dad Brendan walked out of the family home on Darren's tenth birthday. But it would be harsh to blame him for choosing to leave on this day. When he woke up that morning, he hadn't planned to go. The thoughts in his head which had been telling him he wasn't worthy of being called 'dad' anymore had simply got the better of him.

For almost 2 years Brendan had been out of work. He used to earn a living as a garage mechanic but he had injured his back in an accident at work, which meant he could no longer work on the cars. After applying for a series of jobs to which he was patently unsuitable, but which personal desperation left him no choice, he considered his prospects bleaker than they had ever been. He couldn't see how he could be of any benefit to his family anymore. He just couldn't see how his family might need him. Yet they did desperately need him. In the first place, they needed his benefits cheque. Darren's mother also needed Brendan to look after Darren and his sister when she went out to look for work. They needed his physical presence in the home to boost family morale. Darren's mum needed the company of another adult in the house to help shoulder the mental load of being the only breadwinner.

And Darren desperately needed a father figure. But Brendan didn't see it like that. He just felt worthless, and so he got up and went as far away as he could get on one £20 note. A few months later Darren's mum, whose mental health had always been bad, began experiencing suicidal thoughts. (She already suffered chronic asthma and diabetes.)

After finishing primary school, where he says he learnt to read and write, Darren spent three more months at secondary school before he started to take days off to look after his sick mum. He was absent more times than he was present until he didn't bother going back at all. The school teacher alerted the part-time truancy officer who in turn tried to bring him back. Calls to Darren's home went unanswered. When the truancy officer rang the social services department, she was told there weren't enough staff to go round to check on him. The truancy officer did ring back the next week to discuss what else she and the social services could do to get Darren back to school, but no one picked up the phone. When they finally spoke a month later, the conversation didn't go well. Although Darren's mother was suicidal, and Darren was at risk himself, the case did not meet the 'seriousness' threshold required for any action to be recommended. So the truancy officer spoke to the teacher. But because the teacher had only known Darren for 2 months, her opinion was discounted as not being 'evidence based'. No help was forthcoming and Darren didn't ever go back to school.

In the meantime Darren made himself useful looking after his little sister on Fridays, Saturdays and Sundays when his mum was well enough to go to work at the local chippy. The pay was poor but she was usually able to bring home cold fish and chips for the children, which they heated up. The only trouble was that when she was feeling too ill to go to work she didn't get paid or bring home supper. Darren's mum had tried to apply for state benefits to help get through the difficult weeks, but the DWP interviewer had judged the cold fish and chips to count as tips and so added them to her wages. It meant she exceeded the minimum income requirements to qualify for a proper entitlement; instead she was awarded £25 a week. When Darren's mum tried to challenge this ludicrous interpretation of her situation, the 'local' DWP office 10 miles away called her in for an interview.

On the day of the interview, Darren's mum was having one of her very bad days and couldn't travel to town. The family situation was becoming increasingly precarious. Darren and his sister got used to going without food for days. Household services were routinely cut off as his mother's meagre benefits were reduced when she frequently failed to meet the terms of the pledges she had made to the DWP-appointed 'work coach'. Darren was sent to the local food bank or on raids to the supermarket bins. When he had no joy there, he started to beg on the street.

Darren isn't a one-off case. There is plenty of evidence that the scourge of destitution has returned to the council estates and isolated rural settlements of Britain. Destitution is defined in two ways: experience of at least two of six poverty measures over the previous month, including eating fewer than two meals a day for two or more days; or a weekly income after housing costs of £70 for a single adult or £140 for a couple with children. This is defined as an income level below which people 'cannot meet their core material needs for basic physiological functioning from their own resources'.

An estimated 1.5 million people in the UK, including 350,000 children, experienced destitution in 2017.[1] The desperation of families like Darren's have shocked seasoned professionals – the doctors, social workers and lawyers who have to pick up the pieces of these broken lives. As the Labour MP and anti-poverty campaigner Frank Field said at the time of the 2017 destitution findings: 'Clearly something unique and horrendous is happening to the bottom end of our society'.

The shocking scale of destitution is now being confirmed in other data. A recent Oxford University study[2] carried out for the Trussell Trust found that 80 percent of people using food banks regularly went whole days without food. Average household income for this group was £319 a month; one in six reported no money coming in at all over the previous 4 weeks. A separate study by Christians Against Poverty found similar levels of deprivation: families going without food, toiletries or even beds, while locked into high-cost credit, reliant on food handouts and subjected to dangerous levels of stress.[3]

Darren Reid and his family partly dealt with their poverty by moving homes. Once they had racked up housing debt with one council they reapplied for emergency housing at another. But one consequence of this council welfare shopping was that Darren's mum could no longer claim benefits. She had been forced by her bleak circumstances to break every repayment or work agreement she had ever made with the DWP and the council. Now, she had come to the end of her tether.

When Darren was 18 years old, his mum took her own life. As Darren says: 'I think she decided to end it because being alive was so fucking expensive'.

★★★

There is evidence that so-called deaths of despair in Britain have more than doubled since the early 1990s.[4] Those who don't die by their own hand are incrementally brought down by a never-ending battle with their finances. New evidence suggests more than 130,000 deaths in England between 2012 and 2017 could have been prevented if improvements in public health policy had not stalled.[5]

The study by the Institute for Public Policy Research (IPPR) think tank found that during the 1990s and 2000s there was a continual decline in deaths of smokers, drinkers, drug users and other people exposed to poor health risks. But this progress came to a shuddering halt in 2012. If it hadn't, over 130,000 deaths may have been avoided. Part of the reason for this stark reversal of the health fortunes for the most disad-vantaged was a decade of austerity, slashing the public health, prevention and mental health budgets of the NHS, as well as wider national and local government services which have an impact on preventable diseases.[6]

Darren wasn't able to attend his mum's funeral. Her funeral arrangements were financed and organised by the local council. Every year thousands of so-called pauper's funerals take place unnoticed at crematoria across the country. The service is very basic: a coffin and the services of a funeral director to bear the body to the crematorium 'with dignity'. There is no money for flowers, viewings or obituaries in the local paper. The only burials permitted are those in unmarked shared graves. For Darren and his little sister, there wasn't even any money to cover their transport costs, so they walked to the crematorium. It took them so long that they were too late for the 5-minute ceremony. Darren still doesn't like to talk about the day he missed his own mum's funeral.

Darren's mum died with just £38 in her Post Office account, money which was taken by the council as a token payment towards the full funeral cost of £1,700. After his mother's death Darren spent 18 years in and out of local authority accommodation. At one time he was holding down a part-time job as a scaffolder until he got whacked on the head with a scaffolding pipe. The company gave him £100 and told him not to bother coming back. He spent that £100 on an 'amazing buzzing week' of bingeing on booze and soft drugs, culminating in a drunken fall down an escalator in a shopping centre. Ever since then he's been on some form of benefits and in and out of mental health treatment centres.

He appears haunted more by his mother's life than her death. He knows only too well just how important it is not to fall off the government radar, not to break the trust of the multitude of government agencies he has negotiated with over the years. Darren has adapted and acquired some personal tools to help him work the system. He smiles a lot and makes promises about how he intends to tackle his problems, most of which, to his credit, he keeps. His defence against destitution is his affability. But it hasn't always been enough. So Darren has had to supplement his benefits with the begging he learnt as a kid.

He used to beg near cashpoints until the council made it a criminal offence. Local governments have now instituted a more ironic punishment than an eighteenth-century flogging: these days, beggars receive a fine. Councils like West Suffolk has issued banning orders against anyone sitting with a receptacle with an intention to beg. Welwyn Hatfield Council has given its officers the power to fine people sitting on the ground 'inviting donation'. What does it say about a society and its attitude towards money when we criminalise people who sit too near to cashpoints? Are some people not even allowed *near* money? Fining people who are already so desperate that they are willing to risk public opprobrium is pointlessly cruel.[7] But the unthinking rush to move to a cashless society is even more insidious because it robs the poorest of the option of appealing directly to their own community for charity. What's the point of proffering a begging bowl if there is nothing to put in it?

Darren's girlfriend, Stacey, spent her teenage years in children's homes after her parents split up, and neither her mum nor her dad wanted to look after her. She has been diagnosed as suffering from scleroderma, a connective tissue disorder and autoimmune disease that causes the skin to thicken and then slowly darken. Stacey's condition has spread internally to her heart, kidneys and lungs. Eventually her organs will start to fail. The cause of this disease is unknown and there are also no known scientific means of prevention, so the mortality rate for those with advanced stages of scleroderma is high. Up to now Stacey has learnt to live with the illness and uses cosmetics to disguise the effect it is having on her skin, although she says it feels like her face is being gripped by a 'tight evil mask'. She is in receipt of £600 a month in disability benefits through the Personal Independence Payment (PIP) scheme.

Since leaving the children's home she has been through a number of traumatic and abusive relationships with men. Nearly all of her 'boyfriends' have financially abused her by pressuring her to give them her benefits. Stacey says Darren is the first who hasn't taken advantage of her in that way. But neither of them has much money at the best of times, and she has taken to supplementing her benefits by working a couple of times a week as a prostitute. She uses an online brothel run by a man whom Darren once owed money to. Darren was released from the debt on condition he introduced the man to Stacey. She did her 'first job' after she failed a PIP assessment meeting at which the (non-medically qualified) medical assessor doubted the effects of her disability on her everyday life. She was awarded just five PIP points. The qualifying minimum is 11. It meant her benefits were temporarily stopped until she had the decision overturned on a mandatory reassessment. Now, when she sees clients, the brothel takes half of her fee. Because of her condition, Stacey finds the work painful, and when her condition flares up she is forced to cancel 'appointments' at short notice.[8]

In October 2019 a parliamentary report found a strong link between prostitution and benefit sanctions where women on Universal Credit have to sell sex on the streets to make up money docked from their state allowances or while waiting for delayed payments.[9] Between 2010 and 2017 on-street prostitution in the UK rose by 60 percent, a large part of which can be attributed to women failing to meet the strict tests set by the benefits system. Changing Lives,[10] a charity that provides women's services across the North of England and the Midlands, conducted research in 2016 into what it termed 'survival sex work'. It found women to be selling penetrative sex for £10, for a place to stay or even in exchange for clean clothes, with 'punters' approaching them to offer as little as a fiver at times when the women are perceived as being particularly vulnerable. Some of the women complained that they were only on the streets because they'd had their benefits stopped for missing job-centre appointments or failing to attend interviews.

Laura Seebohm, the director of operations at Changing Lives, says:

We noticed a big increase in women selling sex after the introduction of benefit sanctions, not just to make ends meet but, in some cases, to provide the basics for their family. Some of the women were so desperate that they were selling sex for the first time while others had successfully got themselves out of the world of survival sex only for the sanctions to come along and force them back into it.[11]

Darren hates what Stacey has to do to survive, but he is in no position to help. At least he is still on the old benefits system. It means he has yet to negotiate the reforms brought in by the new Universal Credit scheme. Universal Credit is a benefit for working-age people, merging six benefits into one payment: income support, income-based job-seeker's allowance, income-related employment and support allowance, housing benefit, child tax credit and working tax credit. The idea was to make claiming benefits simpler and encourage people on low incomes to find full-time work.

MPs sitting on the Work and Pensions committee who looked at the new system have concluded that Universal Credit is actually making it harder to live and harder to get into full-time work.[12] They have linked the scheme to increased debt, rent arrears and food bank use. The MPs stated:

The introduction of Universal Credit is causing unacceptable hardship and difficulties for many of the claimants it was designed to help... However, while the Department is responsive to feedback on its digital systems from staff, it has persistently dismissed evidence that Universal Credit is causing hardship for claimants and additional burdens for local organisations, and refuses to measure what it does not want to see.

It is hard to understand why ministers can't see these obvious failings – half of all DWP staff working in job centres are dependent on benefits.[13]

This nation-wide transfer from the old system to Universal Credit has meant that 1.9 million people lost at least £1,000 a year, while 1.6 million gained at least £1,000.[14] The bill for bringing in this seismic reshuffling of national benefits is £12 billion. But already it has been those with the lowest incomes who have lost the most. The government did set aside £3 billion to ease this process, but new claimants won't benefit from the protection and if people's circumstances change – for instance, if they come off benefits and then go back on them – they lose this transitional protection. This is hardly surprising since the driving philosophy was not one of support but of saving the government money.

What is coming down the tracks is quite terrifying. The government expected 11 million people to be on Universal Credit, yet by the end of 2019 just 2.6 million people had claimed it.[15] Most of those on the old system, like Darren, are dreading the changeover and will do anything they can to avoid it. In Harrogate, Yorkshire, the region where millions of pounds were ploughed into a pilot system guaranteeing claimants will be no worse off after transfer, the take-up rate has been low. Yet under the 'change of circumstances' trigger the transfer process has been made ludicrously easy to initiate. A claimant who reports having a new boyfriend or girlfriend, or even a modest pay cut at work, can trigger an automatic transfer. And once you have started you can't go back, even when a claimant realises he or she was better off on the old benefits. Perhaps uniquely among government bureaucracy, if a claimant enters incorrect answers when making a transfer, the DWP will not deny the claim. Demonstrably impossible answers to the questions, like ticking a box to say you have 99 children or putting the moon as your place of residence, won't derail a transfer to Universal Credit. Nor does a claimant require any identification documents, an address or even a bank account. The form itself is just 3 pages long, where the old housing benefit form ran to 45 pages.

Perhaps the strangest part about the benefits system is that Darren Reid will end up receiving more money in state handouts and public services than most people ever earn in a lifetime. In fact, Darren's 'earnings' put him in the top 20 percent of all incomes. He is only thirty-five and has worked no more than a handful of days in his life – yet his cost to the country is already around £1 million. The prognosis is one of downward spiral: sucking in more welfare benefits, assessments, emergency call-outs and medical treatment and prescribed drugs worth double what has already been spent. It will end up costing £3 million that needn't have been spent. If we had invested in Darren when things started to go wrong, the state could have saved a fortune.

And Darren is worth saving. As he says: 'I'm pretty bright you know. I can read and write coz I was good at primary school. But I didn't learn anything after that'. He's keen to learn and with a little help early on he could easily have turned his life around. An early intervention at any one of those critical junctures in Darren's life – when his dad left home, when his mum died or when he lost his scaffolding job – would have made economic sense.

Britain's benefits bill reached £100 billion a year in 2019. The financial cost to the country in terms of additional hardship payments made in the wake of the coronavirus means the final figure could be two or three times more.

The average earner pays more than £200,000 of their life-time's taxes on welfare alone.[16] If a social worker had picked up the phone when Darren's truancy officer rang, or if the government had allocated 2 hours of a social worker's time looking into the unreasonable burdens the young Darren had on his shoulders, 15 people could have saved themselves £200,000. More importantly, Darren – and remember there are hundreds of thousands of other 'Darrens' in the UK – could have joined the ranks of the employed, paid his own taxes and made a better life for himself. He may have even become rich.

5

WORKERS

THE MORTICIAN WHO BECAME
A HAIRDRESSER

James Flett left school with a smattering of low-grade GCSEs and an 'A' in art and design. His mum always knew he had 'creative genes' but he always preferred playing football to painting daffodils. Nevertheless, he took his mum's advice and enrolled in a further education college to study a BTEC in hair and beauty. It wasn't long after leaving college that he got a job as a hairdresser in a trendy salon on Guildford high street in Surrey. And for a while he thought it was going to work out:

It was a challenge to start with, but when I could do the basics I soon got bored. It wasn't the cutting and styling so much as the boring talking to the customers that made me think it really wasn't for me. So I gave them 2 months' notice and left with no concrete plans about what to do next.

His mum told him the local hospital was advertising for 'beauticians', although he couldn't imagine what his BTEC and hairdressing experience could mean in a medical context. 'But it did sound intriguing and at least it would be different and perhaps it was something I could do'.

Not for one moment did James think working for the NHS would turn out to be his dream job. When James finished college all he wanted was paid work which left him enough money to go out on the weekend. As it turned out, a hospital in Surrey was looking for beauticians to work in the mortuary. It was a sensitive appointment and so the job advert didn't spell out the nature of the work in black and white. The successful candidate would be someone who could work in a 'challenging environment' and had experience of hospital work. James didn't really have the right experience, but he impressed in his interview and was offered a position pending a probation period:

> During the first week they kept me away from the bodies and stuck me in the office upstairs. I was filing medical forms and family details. It wasn't really using my BTEC or doing what I wanted to do and, to be honest, if anything, it was even more boring than the hairdressers.

At the start of the third week James decided to speak to his boss.

> I just said I wanted to do something that was more hands on. The two mortuary technicians looked at each other and the next thing I know I was in scrubs and being taken down to the mortuary. At first they told me to watch what they were doing and if I felt queasy I should leave the room and grab some fresh air. Apparently everyone feels a bit queasy on their first day.

But James didn't. He watched with absorbing fascination as the two clinicians went about their work brushing the corpse's hair and dabbing the cheeks with rouge ready for the family to come and view the body. James says:

> The skill is in making sure the body is recognisable to the family as the son/daughter/father/wife or whoever they last knew them as. If they happen to have been in a nasty road traffic accident, then you can have your work cut out. But even with head injuries you can still stitch the bits back together again. Then it's all about the clever placement of scarves and hats. You probably have to be a certain kind of person to do this job. But if you don't mind the gore and messy bits, then it can be pretty satisfying. I actually think it is creative, even artistic.

And it certainly gave James something to talk about in the pub.

James had joined the team as a mortuary and bereavement assistant, a job that was graded on the same level as a hospital cleaner. On a starting salary of £16,400 he knew it was going to be tough. The bus to the hospital would cost him £74 a month. On top of that he had to pay rent and all his bills.

The mortuary manager assured him that he wouldn't be stuck on that salary for long. So he just tried to make ends meet the best he could until his salary was increased. But the NHS pay structure is rigid, especially at the bottom. After his first year at the hospital he was called in for his annual appraisal. His managers told him his work was excellent and he was especially praised for his social interaction skills with the families. But the budgets were very tight and no one was getting a pay rise – he must have heard about the 'austerity cuts'. They would see what they could do for him next year.

James was already slipping into debt. After rent, food and council tax he had about £15 to spend on himself at the weekend or use for emergencies. The bank had agreed to an overdraft of £300 but he had borrowed beyond this and was now incurring unarranged overdraft interest at 40 percent. A few weeks after starting he had received a letter from the hospital trust requesting payment for the cost of the police checks carried out by the Disclosure and Barring Service when he had applied for the job. These checks are a mandatory requirement for the employment of anyone who is involved in the handling of sensitive medical records. James had ignored the follow-up reminders and now the trust said he owed £49 and gave him 2 weeks to pay. Even if he didn't go on holiday or denied himself nights out, which he was willing to do, James simply wasn't earning enough to get by. It didn't matter how much he loved his job if he was always broke.

James is among more than 1 million public sector workers in Britain who are paid less than the amount required to make a living, trapping them in in-work poverty. According to The Living Wage Foundation[1] there are as many as 1.2 million people working for the NHS, councils and other public sector employers who receive unsustainably low wages of less than £9 an hour (or £10.55 in London).

Public sector workers, employed either directly by the state or on outsourced contracts, account for up to 20 percent of the 6 million people in Britain who are paid less than the real living wage – the voluntary minimum set each year to reflect true living costs. The real living wage is higher than the government's legally enforceable 'national living wage' which was £7.83 an hour across the country in 2019. The vast majority of public sector workers earning below the real living wage are in local authority jobs. They are our teaching assistants, cleaners, care workers and catering staff. Almost half a million are on outsourced contracts, while another 725,000 work directly for a public sector body.

James first realised he had to do something to arrest his precarious financial position when he found himself hiding in the toilets of the local pub because he was embarrassed about not being able to afford a round of drinks. He knew he shouldn't have accepted the invitation but he wanted to be there – it was the office Christmas party and he had wrongly assumed that his department would put money behind the bar.

After receiving the trust's demand for the background-check fee, James was now forced to look for a second job to top up his salary so he could pay for the cost of his first job. He was insulated from the shock by the knowledge that so many of his friends and colleagues in the hospital had already followed the path of secondary employment.

It may be fashionable to categorise James's plight as in-work poverty. But for many it is just old-fashioned poverty by another name. In some ways it can be a worse experience than surviving in out-of-work poverty. The stress of holding down a job while struggling to keep on top of bills can wear people down such that they are never pulling free from the tugging quicksand of bills and debt.

James found himself staring at the permanent advert in the window of his local newsagent seeking 'late hours staff – minimum wage'. When the owner confirmed how little James would be paid, he shrugged his shoulders tiredly and reasoned with himself that the real convenience of this job was how close it was to his home.

For several weeks the newsagents worked out. James worked all day Saturday and then did a couple of late shifts in the week. He had less time to spend with his boyfriend, Khaled, but it meant he didn't have to leave the job in the hospital mortuary, where he felt proud to be. However, one night when he turned up for his shift the owner was there to meet him. He accused James of failing to properly lock up the night before, which had allowed someone to break in. The owner seemed even more irate because the burglars 'used my carrier bags to carry everything out of my shop'. He was understandably upset and James tried to calm him down. But the owner told James that because he couldn't trust him anymore he would have to let him go. The owner said he was keeping James's wages for the month in compensation for the stolen goods. He said James was lucky he hadn't called the police. James protested his innocence – he must have been tired from his day's work at the hospital – but it made no difference.

James wasn't just back where he started – he was worse off. He had already 'spent' the money he had earned on a new fan heater for his bedroom. His bills were now all coloured red. Whatever he did next to keep himself solvent would be the last throw of the dice. He only earned an extra £110 a week but it was enough to keep his debt at bay. He just needed some emergency cash to bail him out until he found another second job.

James had seen ads for payday-loan companies on one of the hospital noticeboards. He had also read the stories about how they charged extortionate interest and then, when you couldn't pay, sent the heavies round. But James, like so many before him, didn't think this would happen to him. He'd get the loan repaid as soon as he got that second job or a pay rise – whichever came sooner. But that's how the payday-loan industry works. It ensnares customers with small loans, knowing that before long they'll be asking for bigger loans to pay off the last ones, robbing Peter to pay Paul.

The convenience of no credit check scores and a simple online application form attracts millions of workers every year. Customers can even get a quick loan by using an app on their mobile phone.[2] The Financial Ombudsman Service,[3] which handles complaints against the companies, has dealt with customers who held more than 100 payday loans at one time, which tells you everything you need to know about the probity of the fast loans industry. Payday loans accounted for 39,715 of all new complaints handled by the FOC in 2019, marking a 130 percent rise from the year before. Despite new caps brought in during 2015, loan companies continue to thrive on struggling workers who have given up on getting rich and just want to get by. In an unusual side hustle, Uber is now offering a payday-loan service[4] to its hard-up drivers. Presumably it won't be long before Amazon and Deliveroo start taking advantage of their own low-paid captive work forces.

★★★

James is fortunate in that he has a roof over his head. Jasper is not. Jasper is one of the 32.75 million whom the government statistically counts as having a job.[5] He used to live in Edinburgh, where he was working at Amazon's Dunfermline warehouse. But although he was being paid just over the minimum wage, after he deducted the £10 fare for the bus laid on by Amazon for its workers, he was living below the breadline. He soon found he couldn't afford to keep both his room in Edinburgh and his job with Amazon. So Jasper decided to move to Dunfermline.[6] But it turned out rents in Dunfermline were not much cheaper than those in Edinburgh and so Jasper was actually no better off. Then he had a conversation with one of the Amazon workers who had come from Bosnia to look for work. He told him he was saving money while working at Amazon because he didn't pay rent. When Jasper asked where he lived, he told him that he slept in a tent under a bridge just outside the town.

Jasper decided to try it. He would be saving £350 a month, which would soon get him back in the black, and then he could rent a room in town.

Jasper jokes that his new address is convenient for work because he can get to the 'office' in less than 10 minutes. It's also very convenient for his bosses at Amazon who employ him on a zero-hours contract. Amazon doesn't care where he lives. It doesn't matter that he doesn't have an address or a bank account because they can pay him into his mobile phone account. All they care about is that he turns up on time. But now that Jasper is living in a tent he can't claim Universal Credit to supplement his meagre earnings. The DWP have told him that, as he's not paying rent, he actually earns too much.

There are some politicians who appear to think that stories like those of Jasper and James demonstrate that British workers have never had it so good. Before the catastrophic impact of the coronavirus on the economy, employment levels had hit a record high. Three million more of us were working today in the UK than in 2008. So it doesn't seem unreasonable to assume that people who fall out of one job will find another one shortly. As long as you keep getting on your bike, as Norman Tebbit used to say, you will find work. Yet between 2013 and 2018 more than 500,000 British workers were swept into working poverty. Employment has risen, but the number of people in work living below the breadline has risen faster.

In 2018 the number of workers in poverty hit 4 million, meaning about one in eight people across the country is classified as working poor.[7] Nearly all of this increase comes as more and more working parents find it harder to earn enough money to pay for food, clothing and accommodation due to weak wage growth, an erosion of welfare support and tax credits, and the rising cost of living.[8] It's a phenomenon that is troubling politicians of all political colours. The Tory MP Robert Halfon talks about a 'striver's poverty' where a single mother comes home from a low-paid job but can only afford to keep the heating on for a few hours a night. And former Tory MP Rory Stewart, an old Etonian, said that before he stood down from his seat in Cumbria he noticed an increase in working people turning up at his surgery who were struggling with relative poverty.[9]

The paradox of high employment and even higher poverty is hard to reconcile. But there are two drivers which have helped to keep workers on low wages: one is a decade of cuts in benefits directed by policies of austerity, and the other is the insecure nature of new kinds of low-paid work that record numbers of job seekers are taking up.

David Graeber, the author of *Bullshit Jobs*, explains this apparent paradox in terms of the political need for developed capitalist societies to keep people working irrespective of the value of their contribution to the economy. By adhering to a policy of austerity and low paid work the government can point to a massive £37 billion[10] saving in benefits between 2010 and 2020. Just under half the total savings have come from freezing most working-age benefit levels from 2016, a policy which cut nearly £16 billion off the welfare bill. The Tory government has recently declared austerity to be over, but words can't wipe away the long-term consequences of a decade of underinvestment. Even if funding is pumped back into local government, the NHS and the welfare system, it will take a long time to have any impact. For the millions of lives already damaged by austerity, it's too late.

Some of the most disproportionate cuts are in disability benefits – personal independence payments (PIP) and employment support allowance (ESA) – which together will have shrunk by nearly £5 billion[11] (10 percent) since the start of the decade. Such deep cuts to benefits have forced families on to the breadline, and even into prostitution, as we've seen.[12] The stated aim of the austerity programme was to use benefits to help people like Jasper and James keep their jobs. And in one respect it is working: households receiving ever-decreasing benefits have been forced to choose between destitution or finding very low-paid work. Those who still support the policies of austerity will no doubt argue that these kinds of 'tough decisions' made by families at the bottom of the heap is proof that we are 'all in it together'.

Yet few economists predicted that their children and grand-children would be working so hard for so little and at such a personal cost. John Maynard Keynes thought that by now we would be working a 15-hour week.[13] And John Kenneth Galbraith, in *The Affluent Society*, wrote we would be bribing people to give up their jobs or seek early retirement. Instead, people are working longer and harder in jobs that sometimes *cost* more than they pay.

I met James Flett in a barber's shop in 2019. As he cut my hair he told me how much he missed his job in the hospital mortuary:

I wanted to stay but it just didn't make financial sense. I asked them to pay me or offer me some subsidised accommodation but I wasn't getting a response. In the end no one was listening. That was my pay and that was the job. Take it or leave it. So I left.

Sadly, the coronavirus brought more work to the mortuaries of Surrey than they could comfortably cope with. But a system which for decades undervalued and underpaid key workers like James has left the NHS understaffed and ultimately vulnerable to being overrun by a pandemic.

6

RENTERS

THE PRINCESS AND THE PAUPERS

It was a winter's day in Blackpool in early 2019. For once the residents had something to cheer about: the Duke and Duchess of Cambridge had chosen north Lancashire's most famous holiday location as a stop-off on their tour of the nation's less prosperous communities. There were no royal makeovers or celebrity diversions – this was intended as a warts-and-all glimpse of the reality of a fading seaside resort in the North of England. And the town didn't disappoint.

The royal couple must have steeled themselves before they peeked inside a house in Kirby Road carefully chosen for the visit. Years of neglect, damp and leaks had left the ceilings covered with blooms of black mould spores. The wooden floors were sinking into the 150-year-old foundations and the walls were coated in graffiti. Among the scrawled expletives, smiley faces and unknown names there was a shopping list: egg, bread, biscuits, tins…

Kirby Road is just a few hundred metres from Blackpool's famous tower. And the royal reporters, keen to put the visit on a more upbeat footing, asked the Duchess of Cambridge whether she would be spending her time at the seaside to take the royal children to see the famous Blackpool landmark. No she wasn't, 'maybe next time', replied the Duchess.

Today, eight of the ten most run-down neighbourhoods in England are in Blackpool,[1] and overall Blackpool is ranked as the most deprived of 326 local authority areas in England.

Fifty years ago this seaside town had been the jewel in the crown of the northwest's booming domestic tourism. But Blackpool's unplanned response to hordes of seasonal holidaymakers led to a chaotic building bonanza of low-grade housing. When cheap Mediterranean holidays brought about the collapse of the local economy in the 1980s, Blackpool was left with an awful lot of cheap homes, which sucked in low-income families from outside the town looking for affordable accommodation. Those residents who didn't escape Blackpool were stuck in an economic wilderness of low-paid jobs and underinvested neighbourhoods, fuelling a cycle of deprivation. Then came the 1990s recession.

And next the national property prices boom. The first parts of Britain to benefit were the more affluent communities where negative equities were soon eaten up by a rash of gentrification projects. But economically deprived towns like Blackpool, with their abundance of undesirable housing stock, missed the housing boom. In Kirby Road, gradually, house by house, the whole street fell into disrepair.

Judy Storrie, fifty-five, short, dyed blonde hair and friendly, was one of the Blackpudlians who never made it out. She has lived and worked near Kirby Road all her life, mostly employed by the seafront tourist industry, working all the hours she can when there's seasonal work and lying low in the winter. She's been married twice and has four children:

I loved the work when I was young, 'cause you could make a good amount of money, especially if you're single. But when I started having kids and needed more income it became a lot harder, and if the men aren't earning for you it gets even harder. My mum and dad rented round here and their parents rented before them, so we knew the town well and had built up lots of friends and connections.

Judy could never afford to buy her own home, even at Blackpool's more reasonable prices. So she got used to renting. 'At first the landlords were local people who let you rent a top floor of their house', she remembers. 'Then later they sold to other, bigger landlords who ended up owning whole streets. They took in anyone who could pay; they didn't care because they weren't the ones who were living downstairs anymore'. She has complained to the landlord and the council about her living conditions but she says nothing ever gets done. 'They let us live in squalor. I wouldn't even put a rat in here – let alone a pig. It is disgusting'.

The story of Blackpool's decline from candy-floss glamour to economic despair is mirrored in many of Britain's coastal towns. The All Parliamentary Group for Coastal Communities found that seaside towns like Blackpool, Cleethorpes, Scarborough and Hastings have been 'left behind' by the rest of the country. Workers living there earn on average £1,600 less per year than those living inland.[2] This means that, for most, the prospect of owning a home has become unattainable. Instead, bed-and-breakfast rents and council lets dominate the housing landscape.

But the inexorable rise in house prices since the 1990s property boom has also created winners. The property-owning classes are getting rich while the renters are getting poor. In central Blackpool over 80 percent of private tenants, like Judy Storrie, receive housing-related benefits. The same is true in former coastal resorts in the south of the country. Thanet District Council has reported similar figures of 75 percent of private sector tenants in Cliftonville (Dover) being in receipt of housing support.

Social housing rents are kept artificially high by the private-rented sector. An investigation by the National Housing Federation found that of 217 properties for rent in Thanet in 2019, only one was affordable to low-income families on benefits. This combination of rising rents and a government freeze in housing benefit means that, across the country, more than nine out of ten rented properties are unavailable to low-income families.[3] But our housing crisis is not restricted to our seaside towns nor our most neglected communities.

In 2019 a homeless woman in her thirties gave birth to twins on the street outside the gates of Cambridge University's wealthiest college, Trinity (worth an estimated £1.3 billion).[4] In the same year the number of 'households' identified as homeless or at risk of being homeless increased to levels not seen since the start of the 2008 recession. Between April and June 2019, 68,170 households were initially assessed as homeless or threatened with homelessness; of those, 32,220 households were officially homeless – an increase of 23 percent on the year before.[5]

★★★

For families who are lucky to have roofs over their heads the problem may be less critical, but it is no less crushing.

Another 8.4 million people in England are living in an unaffordable, insecure or unsuitable home, according to the National Housing Federation. The housing crisis is impacting all ages across every part of the country. Almost 130,000 children dependent on their parents or carers now live in temporary accommodation, a rise of 83 percent since 2011. These children are drawn from 60,000 households who have no permanent home. More than 7,000 of these are in bed-and-breakfast accommodation, up 3.2 percent between 2018 and 2019. Another 3.6 million people live in overcrowded homes and 2.5 million more simply can't afford their rent or mortgage. A further 2.5 million adults are stuck living with parents, with an ex-partner or with friends, because they can't afford to move out. Almost half (43 percent) of these 8.4 million people can only afford to live decently if they are in social housing. Social housing rents are on average 50 percent cheaper than those charged by private landlords, contracts are more secure and many properties are designed specifically for older people with mobility issues.

Different housing pressures are more prevalent in certain regions. For example, more people in the North of England struggle to afford their rent, while people in the South face overcrowding or living with their parents because they can't afford to move out. Everywhere, affordable homes are becoming increasingly more difficult to get.

The National Housing Federation claims the government disguises the true scale of the social housing crisis by publishing waiting lists that don't reflect reality. NHF says the actual number of people in England who need social housing is 3.6 million – 500,000 more households than on the government's official waiting list.[6]

Even those in well-paid jobs can't compete with the rising tides of our property market. Today four out of ten young adults cannot afford to buy one of the cheapest homes in their area even after they have scraped together a 10 percent deposit. This is because house prices in England have risen by 173 percent over two decades while average pay for 25- to 34-year-olds has grown by just 19 percent over the same period. In 1996, by contrast, 93 percent of those with a deposit who borrowed four and a half times their salary could purchase a home.[7] And taken from the perspective of the 1980s, when Britain was enjoying an economic boom, the disparity between today's first-time buyers has widened considerably.

The Resolution Foundation says that in 1980 the average working family spent 10 percent of their income on housing costs, whereas today it spends 20 percent. In 1980 the average working-age family renting privately spent 12 percent of its income on housing costs. Today it spends almost three times this amount at 35 percent.[8]

Vicky Spratt, who has written a book called *Tenants: Stories of Britain's Housing Shame*, says there are now two classes of people in Britain: those who make money from property and those who don't:

Take my friend with serious inherited wealth, for example. She owns two properties, became a buy-to-let landlord before the age of twenty-five and is able to live the millennial dream of pursuing various unprofitable (but highly Instagrammable) side hustles because of an abundance of passive income. And then, consider my friend without family money. She works full-time, pays close to £1,000 a month for a room in a shared flat and over the Christmas break was forced to deal with an email from her landlord – the person she hands over huge chunks of her income to after tax every month – accusing her of 'talking rubbish' when she alerted him to a foul smell whenever she uses her shower.

The solution might seem obvious: Britain needs to build more homes. Actually, it turns out that the problem is more complex than that. In 1996 there were 660,000 more houses than households. Today that surplus has almost doubled to 1.25 million.[9] So just like the paradox of our in-work poverty crisis, where we have more jobs than applicants, our crisis in housing is not caused by having too few homes. What is happening is that we are building the wrong type of houses in the wrong parts of the country and then selling them to people who don't need them.

Between 2014 and 2016 more than 1.2 million people born in the 1950s acquired a second property – including buy-to-let and overseas properties. This means that one in six baby-boomers now owns a second home – that this multiple property-owning class has grown by 53 percent since 2001, amounting to 5.5 million people with a total value of £941 billion. But since 2003, when overall home ownership across the UK peaked at 58 percent, the number of families owning even *one* home has been steadily falling.

The multiple property ownership has been fuelled by a 'rapid growth' in the number of people buying houses in Britain to rent out with almost 2 million people – the majority being older, higher income and southern – owning buy-to-lets. But there is another paradox: research by the Resolution Foundation (RF) has found that some millennials, for so long cast as a benighted property-deprived class, have also become multiple home owners.

Seven percent of those born in the 1980s were living in households with some additional property wealth by the age of twenty-nine – the same proportion of baby-boomers. 'A substantial and fast-growing proportion of this group [millennials] are still becoming multiple property owners', the RF report says, adding that this fits with a pattern of 'rising property wealth concentration within older cohorts and within the fortunate wealthy minority in younger ones'. The 'surprisingly rapid rise' of multiple property ownership among the young generation, like Vicky Spratt's fortunate friend, could mean that those currently in their thirties may be on the way to similar rates of additional property ownership as today's middle-aged cohorts.[10]

What we need is more affordable housing made available to lower-income families; otherwise, the housing market will continue to feed the demand in profitable second homes and overpriced land. The National Housing Federation, Shelter, Crisis, the Campaign to Protect Rural England and the Chartered Institute of Housing all agree the country urgently requires 340,000 new affordable homes every year, including 145,000 social homes. They are calling on the government to build these social homes by investing £12.8 billion every year for the next decade. (For some time now the government has designated housing as 'affordable' if it is sold at less than 80 percent of its valuation, but that is not necessarily what these housing charities and organisations had in mind.)

The government initially responded by setting the bar high. In 2015 David Cameron promised a nationwide scheme to create 200,000 new homes in England for first-time buyers.

The project was also supposed to support the wider growth and regeneration of towns like Blackpool in the north and Dover in the south. More than £2 billion was set aside for the first tranche of 60,000 dwellings. It was exactly the kind of scheme that the housing charities had been calling for. But in November 2019 the government's own financial watchdog, the National Audit Office, made the astonishing announcement that it could find no evidence of a single house being built under the scheme. What undermined the plan from the outset was the government's failure to factor greed into its affordable property scheme.

Perversely, inert land ownership is the most bankable means of getting rich in the UK today. And so, without a real profit incentive, property developers and house builders just sat on their land waiting for prices to rise. In the past few decades 2 million hectares of public land, worth £400 billion, has been acquired by the private sector.[11] It is the largest appropriation of public land in Europe. Each year more of it is owned by smaller numbers of tycoons and conglomerates, ever reducing the chances of wealth accumulation for everyone else.

Homes, too, have become lucrative, tradable commodities. This is not a peculiarly British problem. The UN special rapporteur for housing, Leilani Farha, has highlighted the devastating consequences of society's tendency to regard property as an asset rather than a place to live. Real estate accounts for nearly 60 percent of the value of all global assets and is now worth $217 trillion − of which 75 percent is residential real estate. This represents more than twice the world's total gross domestic product. On publication of her hard-hitting report, Farha declared:

Housing has been financialised: valued as a commodity rather than a human dwelling, it is now a means to secure and accumulate wealth rather than a place to live in dignity, to raise a family and thrive within a community. Housing has become security for financial instruments – traded and sold on global markets. It has lost its currency as a universal human right.[12]

She went on to warn: 'The pace and extent to which financial corporations and funds are taking over housing and real estate and causing homelessness, displacement and unaffordability is staggering'.

Ultimately, it will require either joint global action or a crash to halt the boom and bring property prices back down to earth. Yet lessons from the housing market corrections of the 2008 recession tell us there is every reason to believe that the response to the 2020 coronavirus economic shutdown will change nothing: prices will recover and the dangers of the overinflated property market will be quickly forgotten.

Farha and the UN want governments to intervene and break the link between homes and profits to ensure markets serve housing need rather than investment priorities. But millions of people's financial security is invested in their homes. This makes it difficult for a government to embark on a radical devaluation programme, since it would deprive families and pensioners of their savings. Which politician is going to stand on a platform promising to make rich people poor?

7

MILLENNIALS

THE TRAVEL AGENT WHO SWAPPED HIS CAREER FOR A WINDSURFER

'Twas the night before Christmas and Alex King was getting ready for bed. Tomorrow was going to be like no Christmas he had ever experienced. The 32-year-old administrative assistant had been asked to spend 8 hours of Christmas Day in the office answering the phones and fielding enquiries for package safaris to the Masai Mara in Kenya.

Alex had never been to Africa, so the 45-year-old director, who would be spending Christmas Day with her family, had given him a crib card and some fact sheets so he could bone up on all the necessary information concerning the travel company's holidays and the special Christmas discounts now being advertised. If he had any problems, he should ring another number she had given him. On no account should he ring her but instead contact a twenty-something colleague who was on call over the Christmas holiday.

Alex is a member of what has been written off as the 'snow-flake' generation, an amorphous mass of young people who were unfortunate enough to have been born after everything started to run out. Yet despite this disparaging characterisation of his generation's fortitude, record numbers of millennials joined Alex for work on Christmas Day. According to the

Trades Union Congress, 1 million people were working on 25 December 2019, a fivefold increase from 2010 and 100,000 more than 2018. Most of them were young people like Alex. They included 88,000 nurses and 55,000 nursing assistants. In the bars, restaurants and hotels, an army of nearly 40,000 chefs, 29,000 kitchen assistants and 33,000 waiting and bar staff spent their Christmas Day catering for the baby-boomer generation, who were generally the only ones who could afford to pay the inflated prices charged on Christmas Day.[1]

Alex recalled:

> Going to work on Christmas Day, and getting double the wage, was a no-brainer. I'm on a zero-hours contract because the work tends to be seasonal and very much demand-led. Most of the time I'm helping very wealthy families choose safari holidays based in luxury accommodation in the Masai Mara and the Serengeti. In the summer it is holidays in villas on Caribbean islands. Talk about rubbing salt into the wounds!

Alex is right to feel cynical. People in their late twenties and early thirties are half as wealthy as those now in their forties were at the same age. Today's thirty-something generation, according to research by the Institute for Fiscal Studies,[2] has missed out on the house price boom and golden-plated pensions. Those born in the early 1980s have an average wealth of £27,000 each, against the £53,000 that those born in the 1970s had by the same age. They are the first post-war generation not to have higher incomes in early adulthood than those born in the preceding decade. Worse still, they will find it harder to amass wealth in the future.

But for Alex and his generation the economic reality of their predicament has already bitten. They have swapped the chance of stable careers and reassurance of firmly plotted pay rises for one or often two badly paid jobs. Alex has also taken a job looking after children at a nearby luxury gym, which offers parents the chance to exercise and play sports without having to worry about entertaining the kids. Employment at the gym is also arranged around a zero-hours contract, so Alex is constantly checking his availability on weekly rotas sent round on WhatsApp to make sure he maximises his working time between the holiday company and the gym:

> Mostly it's OK because the managers at the gym and the travel agents try to give me shifts that don't clash. But even so, at least once a week there is a crisis and I have to turn down one of them or try to get a mate to fill in. I probably do about 40 hours a week and earn enough to pay rent on my two-bedroom flat and, after paying my bills, I have some money left over to go out. In the summer weekends I head to the beach to do some windsurfing.

Alex is 32 years old and has configured his employment to support his lifestyle. He has reconciled himself to the fact that his ambitions of earning lots of money as a research chemist will probably never happen. His degree in biology was a 'big mistake':

> I don't need a degree to do what I'm doing now. You could come straight out of school and do my jobs. What galls me is that I still have a £60,000 student loan to pay off and no real prospect of ever doing it. I think I wasted too many years

after university – not really settling and too much arsing about, having a good time. By the time I got to starting a career in research I was too far behind the curve – my CV looked a mess and I couldn't really cover up for those lost years. The jobs always went to the other applicants who didn't have holes in their CV.

Alex did try to retrain as a teacher but by then he was living on the pay from his two jobs. 'Do you know the starting salary for a teacher? It's £25,000. To take a job like that I'd have to give up my flat and my windsurfer'.

★★★

The story of graduate employment since 2000 is one of rising numbers of graduates being forced to settle for non-graduate jobs. Professors Peter Elias and Kate Purcell at the University of Warwick,[3] who have carried out research in this field, define a non-graduate job as one in which the associated tasks do not normally require knowledge and skills developed through higher education to enable the employee to perform these tasks in a competent manner. Examples include receptionists, sales assistants, unskilled factory workers, care workers and home carers. Using this definition of a non-graduate job and focusing on recent graduates who were employed, the percentage of them who were working in one of these roles increased from 36 percent in 2001 to 49 percent in 2017. At the same time Britain's gig economy of unskilled jobs has boomed.

Between 2016 and 2020 the number of people employed in more than one casual job has doubled and now accounts for 5 million workers. That means as many as one in ten working-age adults now rely on steady income from often very precarious work.

The meretricious convenience of logging on to online platforms from the comfort of your home is a convenience that ultimately serves the best interests of companies and not workers. If Alex had been born 10 years earlier, he would have encountered a very different working environment. Instead of being tempted by a bewildering array of temporary or open-ended work, he would have found a much more rigid structure of employment for recent graduates. The opportunity to take a couple of jobs that pay more than a starter salary in a profession or trade was simply unavailable or restricted to labouring and seasonal farm work. But today the work culture of the casual seasonal fruit picker also defines the character of millions of other jobs that used to be performed by a unionised work force.

The growth of zero-hours contracts has gone hand in hand with the growth in the gig economy, sucking in more and more millennials. By not paying sick, holiday and maternity entitlements, global corporate giants like Uber and Amazon have saved hundreds of millions of pounds. But they have made even more money from being able to structure their business around a 'flexible' (that is, dispensable) work force. Fast growing companies like Deliveroo, which has grown to be worth $4 billion using freelance delivery riders, have been quick to take advantage of the more relaxed working climate. This is especially so in the South of England where there's more disposable income to spend on the convenience of a door-to-door fast-food delivery.

Dan Martell, twenty-six, was a Deliveroo rider in Brighton who had worked for the company for 2 years:

For the first year it was a bit of an adventure. It was possible to make a comfortable, if not particularly high, level of living. It was the summer of 2016, there weren't too many other Deliveroo cyclists around, and I was picking up £10 to £12 an hour. I was able to start paying off my overdraft. It was flexible, you could earn money, or take a day off; it was really good.

But then Dan suffered a knee injury and was off work for 3 months. 'There was no sick pay from Deliveroo. I got a bit of Statutory Sick Pay and my grandparents gave me £50 a week, but it soon became a beans-on-toast life.[4]

When he went back to work he found a lot of the couriers were struggling:

Loads of the orders were going to the scooter guys. One ice-cold day in February 2017 there were twenty of us waiting outside all day for orders. In the end I earned just £4 that day. I've had to get side jobs on building sites and pubs. I switched from bike to scooter with Deliveroo and started getting more drops. It was brilliant again. Then I got hit by a car. It was months before I was able to work again. Above all, it's a very precarious living.

But it is not just dynamic service industry companies who are using digital employment platforms and informal employment structures to take advantage of a casual work force.

Zero-hours-contracts work culture is spreading into the mainstream public sectors. Since 2013 the number of NHS workers who report being employed on a zero-hours contract has increased fourfold.[5] More than 30,000 NHS workers are now employed on zero-hours contracts. The true number is likely to be higher as the statistics do not include outsourced workers, or workers employed through controversial wholly owned subsidiary companies that are not bound by nationally agreed employment standards.

Zero-hours contracts have made millions of millennials and older workers vulnerable to debt and homelessness. Nearly 1 million workers a year have had shifts cancelled at less than 24 hours' notice and 600,000 have been threatened with losing shifts if they turn down work.[6]

Twenty years ago employees knew exactly what their monthly pay packets contained and were able to budget accordingly. But today three-quarters of all workers do not receive the same pay from one month to the next. Sudden and volatile shifts in monthly pay have left people teetering on the edge of chronic financial crisis. This volatility is particularly acute among the lowest earners and their income is more likely to fall than that of better-paid people.

Researchers for the Resolution Foundation found that workers who experienced a wage cut typically lose £290 (more than the average monthly grocery bill).[7] For those who made less than £10,000 a year, the average was £180, which represented an even greater fall in income. The think tank said this was likely to lead to 'increased anxiety and stress as well as more debt, and fewer opportunities to save for the future'.

Alex is now reconciled to never owning his own home – it is not only way beyond his current means, but he doesn't rate his chances of ever having the opportunity. Alex's father first bought his house in 1973 when he was 29 years old. He had just moved to Southampton and his job as a university professor paid him around £6,000 a year. The house cost £9,000. As Alex says:

> I am 2 years older now than my dad was then. I earn less than
> he did [after adjusting for inflation] and the average home
> in Southampton is around £300,000. My father's first house
> cost him 18 months of his salary. My first house will cost
> more than 12 years of mine.

House prices have surged at the same time as young people's incomes have faltered. That has enriched the baby-boomers and Generation X, who have staked their claim on the property ladder, but made it very hard for young people following on. Homes suitable for first-time buyers are snapped up by buy-to-let Rachman landlords while property developers sit on land for years until the price is high enough to start building. At the same time property investment firms who promise to allocate affordable homes in luxury developments routinely renege on their obligations without fear of being held to account by local authorities. All this means that many millennials can't even afford to buy a garden shed.

These trends – together with student debt and meagre pensions – seem to be having a psychological impact on millennials and the generation trailing after them. Perhaps because life seems more uncertain, they have become more risk-averse in the labour market. They are less likely to try for long-term careers or move regions for work than previous generations were at the same age. These younger generations have subconsciously opted out of trying to get rich because they can see before them the huge attainment gap between what they can have and what they desire.

Many millennials in the UK have given up on capitalism as a system that promises riches, or even a reliable income, in return for hard work. In the 2019 general election Labour, which campaigned on a radical redistribution of national wealth, had a 43-point lead over the Conservatives among voters aged 18–24 years. (The Conservative share actually fell eight points among this group.) The Conservatives only won because they had a 47-point lead among those aged 65+ years (among whom Labour's vote share fell by 8 points).[8]

Similarly, in America, more than half of millennials want to live in a socialist (52 percent) or communist (6 percent) society. Conversely, only 40 percent want to live in a capitalist one.[9]

Ultimately, it doesn't matter that this generation may be richer in consumption terms than their parents. What's the point of passing down a digital toaster to your own kids?

8

GRAFTERS

THE CITY TRADER WHO LIED
ABOUT HIS HOLIDAYS

Simon Diamond, thirty-five, has a high-powered job in the City working as an assistant broker. His friends and family regard him as a success and tease him about his flash new Mazda and his golfing holidays in Tenerife. But not all is what it seems. Simon left school with five GCSEs and two A levels. After a year out picking and stomping grapes in the vineyards of New South Wales, Australia, he came back to the UK and took a job as a sales clerk at a firm of currency traders. Because he joined at the very bottom, where he was paid a little over the minimum wage, he is not earning the big bucks people think he is. Simon, being the bloke he is, plays up to this image. But his holidays are more Costa del Sol than the Caribbean and the Mazda is being paid off on the never-never.

Which is why he's still working hard and dreaming big. Simon would like the world to see him as the next Gordon Gekko, a City whiz kid with the world at his feet, although the reality is he spends his working week sitting in an office filing transactions executed by the much-better-paid brokers. Five years ago he applied for a job as assistant broker and got it. His salary jumped to £46,000 but his day job didn't really change much, only now he is working even longer hours. Still, he did have some spare cash to splash about which he spent on weekends away and nights out with the boys.

That all changed when he married Tessa, whom he met at an office party. She was a receptionist earning £27,000 a year at an insurance company. Their pooled incomes meant they could afford a large mortgage on a small house, though not in London where they had both grown up. They had to move down the commuter line to the 'gin and Jag belt' of Buckinghamshire where they bought a two-bedroom house on the outskirts of Gerrards Cross. Soon Tessa fell pregnant, with twins, and the Diamonds had suddenly become a family.

As Simon recalled, 'It was a wonderful time and I remember feeling so fulfilled. But overnight our finances had changed and the problem was we didn't really appreciate it'.

Tessa took extended maternity leave and then decided she didn't want to return to work, leaving the family reliant on Simon's £46,000 salary. This single salary had to cover the £500 monthly mortgage, the £930 council tax bill and Simon's annual £3,000 railway season ticket. Then there was the car to ferry the kids around and drive Simon to the station. (The Mazda went the day after they got back from their 'second' honeymoon.) They opted for a finance deal on a new VW Tiguan so they wouldn't have to worry about garage bills or breaking down on the motorway when they visited Tessa's parents, who had retired to Cornwall.

'Things, the bills, our other outgoings like new furniture, the pub and the pictures, were all out of control', says Simon. 'We were bleeding money and we couldn't find a way of stopping it'.

Within a year they had maxed out their credit cards and were rowing about where Tessa should shop for the weekly groceries (Waitrose is nice, but Tesco is cheap). Tessa was forced back to work and took a job as a receptionist/sales executive at a car rental centre. But her salary barely covered the childcare costs. After more rows, they went cap in hand to Tessa's parents and asked to borrow some cash to plug the gap. It was only ever going to be a temporary fix, and when that money ran out they went to the bank for a loan.

They have now put their house up for sale. When they bought the property they could only afford an interest-only mortgage, so they have never paid a penny off the mortgage debt. House prices had risen a little since they made their purchase, but any equity in the sale was swallowed up in conveyancing fees. Simon let his friends think they were moving because they needed a bigger house for the kids. But they ended up renting a two-bedroom flat in town above a Turkish barbershop.

Simon and Tessa's story seems at odds with what we are told about working hard and living well in a prosperous capitalist society. If we put the hours in, then the rewards are supposed to follow. We have already learnt how this bargain no longer works for the low-paid worker trapped in a zero-hours contract where life has become little more than survival. We have discovered that those who are born too late have been barred from the property-owning class and stuck getting by on capped incomes from the gig economy. But Simon works in the City and is on a reasonable salary with the prospect of regular pay rises, bonuses and 6 weeks of holiday. So why do Simon and Tessa appear just as trapped as the shift workers employed in the Amazon warehouse up the road in Bedford?

Simon suspects that the mistake he made was not going to university, not making the decision to study for a degree that could open a door to a profession. He has often seen lesser men and women win promotion over him purely on the basis of a piece of paper awarded after a 3-year booze up in a provincial city. But he's wrong.

***

Asif Munaf was 5 years old when he first realised he wanted to be a doctor. But growing up in one of the most educationally deprived areas in the country, he thought that this was just youthful precociousness rather than a realistic career path:

> My father instilled in us an acute sense of worth and self-actualisation. He often remarked, 'This life you have is not yours. It has been entrusted to you by God, so you have no right to do anything other than your best'. Indeed, it is human nature to look after someone else's possession better than yours. Armed with this timeless pearl of wisdom, I went on to medical school with a renewed sense of obligation.[1]

Asif spent 6 years at med school and a further 7 years of specialist training. He made huge sacrifices along the way, missing out on spending more time with his wife and their young child.

'Having such little time forces you to be creative in the way you spend time with loved ones, so even 15 minutes of uninterrupted time each evening can be worth its weight in gold'.

In November 2019 he was watching BBC TV's *Question Time* when he heard a remark from a member of the audience that cut him to the quick.

Rob Barber, a 38-year-old IT consultant and high-profile motorcycle racer, had taken issue with Labour's then shadow justice secretary, Richard Burgon, over his party's policy of imposing higher taxes on anyone who earns over £80,000, which represents the top five percent of earners.

Mr Barber protested: 'Every doctor, every accountant, every solicitor earns more than that; that's not 5 percent!'

Asif knew differently. He was so incensed by the claim that he logged on to his Twitter account to hit back at the IT consultant's comment: 'I spent 6 years at med school and a further 7 years of specialist training and I get paid £48,000. He needs to #factscheck and use some of his £80,000 on a new shirt and trim'.

To ram home his point he even published his last month's payslip online.[2]

It is true that the average pay of a doctor across the country has reached £80,000, but that includes specialists and those doing private medicine. Many more like Asif, who are well established in their careers, aren't earning anything like that amount. A decade of austerity and pay caps in the public sector have left pay levels for doctors being eroded by as much as 30 percent. In fact, in 2018 the median earnings of general practitioners dropped by £10,000 from the year before. Today two-thirds of doctors believe that they are not paid a fair day's wage, although younger doctors are more dissatisfied than their older, higher-earning colleagues.[3] Perhaps that shouldn't surprise us: the British Medical Association says that junior doctors, often making life-and-death decisions, have a starting salary of little more than £30,000.[4]

It was not just doctors who were tarred by the *Question Time* £80,000 brush. Mr Barber repeated another popular misconception: all lawyers are fat cats. Again this rather superficial assessment of a profession, which is far from homogenous, belies some awkward economic realities.

Take barrister William Gover, for instance. When his grandmother died she left a small legacy to enable him to study for the Bar exam. But 4 years after qualification William says he sometimes makes less money than a McDonald's worker. He receives a flat fee of just £46.50 for daily prosecution work. When he adds in travelling time, overheads for his legal chambers, plus the hours taken to actually prosecute a case in court, he can earn as little as £7.75 an hour. The national minimum wage for workers over twenty-five is £8.21.

Legal experts have warned that the meagre pay handed to young criminal law barristers threatens the rule of law. Such is the scale of the discontent that defence lawyers have organised wildcat strikes as part of their own 2-year campaign against cuts to legal aid rates for Crown Court trials. Now barristers instructed by the Crown Prosecution Service are also claiming that their flat fee for 'standard appearances' at Crown Court hearings is pushing them to the financial brink.

William, a 31-year-old barrister based at 3 Temple Gardens chambers in London, says gross fees paid to him and his colleagues do not properly account for an average of 2 hours of travelling time to and from court and at least an hour of waiting time once they arrive. 'Cuts to the court system mean that the administration of the lists does not run smoothly and therefore cases often do not start when they are listed', he told *The Times*. The flat fee for an average case also includes an hour of actual advocacy before the judge and jury in court.

William's story is by no means exceptional. A blog run by Young Legal Aid Lawyers (YLAL) has attracted many similar stories.

Juliet Caters is a defence solicitor, working on the other side of the case to William. As a newly qualified solicitor her salary is £19,000. She says:

> Depending on what is in the diary, I may be leaving my house at any time from 6am onwards for prison visits, disciplinary hearings or parole board hearings. These visits are very regular and take up significant time due to extensive travelling. If I am office-based for the day, I usually arrive at 8:30am to take advantage of the quiet time before the phone starts ringing.
>
> It is not unusual to have to cover appointments or see clients when they attend the office outside of a prearranged appointment or cover client meetings when the assigned solicitor is otherwise engaged. This typically means having to get 'on top of the papers' in a very quick space of time to be able to take instructions and provide solid advice. On a quiet day, which has run according to my diary, I am able to leave the office between 5 and 5:30pm. The out-of-hours call rota for the police stations, late-night client meetings or at-home preparation for the following day usually keeps me working into the evening from the relative comfort of my dining table.

From her £19,000 salary Juliet has to rent a house and pay for a car, which is vital for her work:

> I am compensated on a low level for mileage, but this is paid in arrears, and out-of-office hours. Travelling time

(e.g. setting off at 7:30am for a 9am start) is unpaid and flexi-working is not possible. I have credit card debt which is slowly being chipped away at, but it is difficult to make ends meet with the rising costs of living. It is not unusual to have a fridge that only has milk and cheese in it and, because I am tired, I often don't shop for groceries. The risk of buying a lot of groceries and being unable to afford to fuel my car is a very real worry.

Juliet says she loves her work but concedes the pay is 'difficult to stomach'. She is currently applying for a prosecution job, like William's, where she believes her salary will 'double': 'I am deeply saddened by having to leave criminal defence legal aid work, but it is now becoming a financial decision'.

There is no doubt that the cuts to legal aid since 2013 have had a devastating impact on access to justice for vulnerable people. The YLAL states:

We are worried that only rich students will be able to afford to pursue a career in legal aid because it will pay so little. This will make the legal aid profession less diverse and will mean that future legal aid lawyers will have little or no personal experience akin to their clients' lives.

But the implications are far more serious than this. If people cannot afford to pay for a lawyer, they will be less able to find anyone to represent them in court. So it becomes a financial trade-off for defendants who have to decide between accepting the punishment or using savings to pay the fine or investing in legal help to avoid a financial penalty, community service or prison time (all of which impact earnings to lesser and greater degrees). As we shall see in the next chapter, these kinds of budgetary calculations have very little to do with any noble ideal of justice and everything to do with how much justice you can afford. Rich people just pay the fines or pay for a privately funded specialist barrister to represent them. When did the quality of justice in this country begin to correlate so shamelessly with the defendant's means? And what is so wrong with enriching lawyers and doctors who serve the public, especially if they are working very long hours and making personal sacrifices to keep people alive or out of prison?

9

TAXES

THE SINGLE MOTHER ON BENEFITS WHO WENT TO PRISON AND THE OLIGARCH WHO DIDN'T

Melanie Woolcock is a single mother who lives with her teenage son in Porthcawl, a seaside town with a population of 16,000 located halfway between Swansea and Cardiff. Melanie works as a sales assistant in the town's sports shop. Economists classify Melanie as a part of the 'DE' socioeconomic group described as 'semi-skilled/unskilled manual occupations, unemployed and lowest grade occupations'. In Porthcawl one in three people are 'DE', a fifth are on benefits and a third have no academic qualifications at all. Only a third of the residents own their own homes. Melanie lives in a two-bedroom property in a modern development in the centre of town. Her council tax is £874.48 a year.

But in 2009 Melanie suffered a severe bout of depression and had to give up her job. She was granted child benefits. But very quickly she struggled to pay her food and energy bills and drifted into financial difficulty. Forced to choose between paying her council tax bill or looking after her family she just 'put her head in the sand' while chalking up £4,742 in council tax debts.[1] In 2014 Bridgend Council issued her with a summons to appear before the local magistrates' court for failure to pay her property tax, though she was unable to attend.

At a later court date she agreed to pay £10 a week towards her arrears, although the magistrates accepted that, at that rate, it would take her 11.5 years to pay off the council debt. Melanie, who couldn't afford to instruct a lawyer, kept up the payments for a few months but eventually defaulted and was sentenced to 81 days of imprisonment in her absence. (It would have been longer but the magistrates knocked off 4 days for the amount she had already paid.) A note of the hearing made by the court clerk simply read:

> Suffers with depression. Has been working part-time in a sports shop in Porthcawl. Buried head in sand. Single parent with very limited means. Current income. Child Tax Credit and Child Benefit. £200 per week. Not well enough to work. She is going to apply for benefits. Min offer £5 per week.[2]

On 5 August 2016, fearing the worst, Melanie had made an eleventh-hour payment of £100. But 3 days later bailiffs and two police officers turned up at her home, where she was arrested and marched off to Bridgend Police Station and then to HMP Eastwood. One can only imagine the anguish she must have felt when she phoned her mother from prison to ask her to break the news to her son that she wouldn't be able to pick him up from school.

'I was being treated exactly the same as someone who had murdered somebody', she said after her release. 'But when you're in there and you feel you haven't committed a crime, you feel a vast injustice being done to you'.

The law says you should only face jail time over council tax for 'wilful neglect or wilful refusal' to pay, not because you can't afford to keep up with payments. But Melanie Woolcock is one of 305 people sent to prison between 2013 and 2019 in England and Wales for failing to pay their council tax. Another 6,278 people were handed suspended sentences for the same offence in that period.

In Knightsbridge, central London, far, far away from Melanie's £206,000 home in Porthcawl, the value of property is measured in millions. This is where Rinat Akhmetov has chosen to set up home. He is Ukraine's richest man, with business assets including coal, steel and telecoms, as well as Shakhtar Donetsk, the football club that was a recent UEFA Champions League contender. *Forbes* magazine has estimated his personal fortune to be $4.6 billion. His penthouse apartment in the palatial Number 1 Hyde Park development in central London is worth a staggering £136 million, once Britain's most expensive private residence.

In terms of lifestyles, Rinat Akhmetov and Melanie Woolcock might as well be living on different planets. Yet they do have one thing in common: the size of their respective council tax bills. Rinat Akhmetov's annual payment of £1,376 is well within touching distance of Melanie Woolcock's £874.[3]

★★★

The rising value or cost of homes, depending on whether you own one or want to buy one, has become Britain's greatest barrier to getting rich. Yet the taxing regime in the UK is unfairly weighted in favour of those who own the most expensive property. While Melanie Woolcock's council tax bill has effectively forced her into debtors' prison, Rinat Akhmetov's council tax burden on his £136 million penthouse is infinitesimal – even, you might say, beneath notice, since most of the extraordinarily wealthy residents of Number 1 Hyde Park haven't even bothered to pay it.[4]

This absurd disparity in tax burdens is playing out across the country, where wealthy homeowners are asked to contribute disproportionately less than those in dire financial need.

Although the Valuation Office Agency is responsible for working out which council tax band each home should fall into, it does not decide what those charges should be. That's up to individual councils.

Despite boasting some of the world's most expensive homes, London boroughs, including Westminster and Wandsworth, have some of the UK's lowest council tax bills. No property in Westminster in 2017 could be charged more than £1,376.28 a year. But for low-paid tenants, council tax, which rose by 57 percent in real terms at the start of the noughties, is often the bill that breaks the family budget.[5]

In 2018 there was over £3 billion of outstanding council tax debt (excluding fees), an increase of a third in just 5 years. Today an estimated 2.2 million households, one in ten of all those liable to pay council tax, are behind with their payments.[6] Missing an average council tax payment of £167, in the first month of the financial year, can escalate to a debt of over £2,065 in just 9 weeks. That's because when someone falls behind on their council tax bill, they become liable for the rest of their annual bill after only 2 weeks. Two types of fees are then added on top of the original tax debt: court costs (typically £84) and bailiff fees (£310).

Council tax arrears is now the most common debt problem facing Citizens Advice clients. Citizens Advice estimates that over £560 million in fees were added to people's council tax debt in 2016–17 alone. This includes £300 million of bailiff fees, which is particularly concerning as some of these fees have to be paid by the person in debt before any council tax arrears can be recovered by the local authority. While financial pressure on councils means they are increasingly reliant on council tax to fund local public services, stretched household finances means more people are struggling to keep on top of their essential bills, including council tax.[7]

The UK is exceptional in that, among the Organisation for Economic Co-operation and Development (OECD) countries, it has the second highest proportion of gross domestic product taken in property taxes and the largest proportion of property tax revenue collected by central government for its own use. The UK also has a relatively high proportion of taxation, close to half, levied on residential property.[8] At the height of the Poll Tax riots in 1990, alternative property taxes, such as the community charge and then the council tax, was presented as progressive taxation. But the system is based on property values that are nearly 30 years out of date.

Britain's council tax is illustrative of the structural unfairness of our entire taxation system across the economy. As a nation today we are taxed more than we have ever been. At 34.4 percent of national income, the tax take is at its highest sustained level since the 1940s. Policy reforms since 2010 have increased tax revenue by about £20 billion overall – despite large giveaways such as increasing the income tax personal allowance, cutting the headline rate of corporation tax and freezing fuel duties. According to the Institute for Fiscal Studies, tax-raising measures, including rises in VAT and National Insurance contribution rates, exceed these tax concessions overall in revenue terms.[9]

We are taxed on our income, taxed on our savings from our income, taxed if we make profits from the investments of our savings and then, once we die, taxed on the money we leave behind. In this way our tax system holds back wealth redistribution and traps workers, even high-earning workers, in well-paid poverty.

But it mostly discriminates against those who cannot afford to pay it.

The principles that underpin taxation in the UK have hardly changed since the first taxes on earnings were formally introduced in 1799. This is particularly so when it comes to the taxation of the British household. In the words of the Income Tax Act of 1806, any income earned by a married woman 'shall be deemed to be the profits of her husband'. Surprisingly this is still the approach to family taxation.

By taxing a married couple in this way, rather than as a family unit, our system fails to recognise the value of unpaid household work and family care that the Office for National Statistics has estimated to be worth £1.24 trillion per year. On average, this means that stay-at-home spouses who cook, clean and wash, and look after and transport children and elderly relatives contribute at least £18,932 of value per person to the national economy each year. The social security system acknowledges the overall economic complexity of a family unit and makes payments and deductions which recognise the financial contribution of the stay-at-home spouse. But although the 'working' spouse benefits from a personal tax-free allowance of £12,500, the 'non-working' spouse is not able to use theirs because for tax purposes they aren't earning any money.

Margaret Thatcher was the first politician who recognised this tax anomaly which she believed held back families. Her Chancellor, Nigel Lawson, proposed allowing the spouse who did not use their personal tax allowance to pass it on to the other spouse. In this way, Lawson argued in his 1985 Budget speech, that income tax worked against a family in which the spouse stayed at home to look after the children:

> It denies to the partners in a marriage the independence and privacy in their tax affairs… There is, therefore, a strong case for changing to a new system of personal allowances more suited to today's economic and social needs. Under this, everyone, man or woman, married or single, would have the same standard allowance; but if either a wife or husband were unable to make full use of their allowance, the unused portion could be transferred, if they so wished, to their partner.

Unfortunately, the transferable allowance scheme was never enacted. The subsequent 1990 Married Couples Allowance didn't come close to doing what Lawson intended for a fair personal allowance transfer scheme.[10]

Jonathan Williams is the Family Policy Officer at Christian Action Research and Education (CARE). He says that by forcing a married couple to be treated as two individuals, the UK tax system fails as good public policy:

> A married couple is not simply two individuals who happen to live together but is a family unit who has committed to one another for life for mutual benefit and self-giving, not individual gain. It makes no sense to treat the family unit as two individuals.

Under this and other anachronistic principles the poorest families in the UK have to pay the highest proportional taxes.

Of course the key word is *proportional*. This means that using the current tax bands – 20, 40 and 45 percent – the lowest earners are hit the hardest and, after paying their taxes, they get to keep proportionally less money. According to CARE research a married couple with one low earner and two children only keep 27 pence for every pound they earn. Under our current tax system we tax the poor as if they were rich.

The reason tax rates for one-earner families with low incomes are much higher in the UK than in other OECD countries is that family responsibility is recognised not within the income tax system, but by means of social security payments that are tapered sharply. Looking back to when independent taxation was introduced in the UK in 1990, the effective marginal tax rate for a one-earner family on 75 percent of the average wage was only 34 percent, close to the OECD average in 2017.

Williams says:

> In the past 30 years, the UK has moved to the strange and illogical position where we tax low-income families, yet we then assume they need propping up with social security payments. This is tantamount to digging holes and filling them in again.[11]

To redress this imbalance we must bring in full transferable allowance schemes which support families – but not just for married couples, for all adults in family unit arrangements. Instead of treating families as financial burdens and holding them back, this reform will help them realise, and for the state to value, their true economic potential.

Of course not all families are treated the same. So we should be also trying to narrow the gap between hard-working families and the super-rich who undermine the tax system by not paying their fair share. Super-rich families simply don't play by the same rules. Or as American billionaire Leona Helmsley famously boasted: 'Only the little people pay taxes'.

In recent years deregulation and globalisation of the finance industry has made it too easy for the super-rich to avoid paying taxes.

In 2019 HMRC data revealed that 9,000 people paid just £5.1 billion in tax on £33.7 billion of capital gains income in the previous year. That works out at an average tax rate of 14.8 percent, lower than the basic rate income tax of 20 percent that people pay on salaries between £12,501 and £50,000. By setting up companies and partnerships to be eligible for lower capital gains tax (CGT) rates and corporation tax, rather than taking earnings, which would be subject to the top rate of income tax, they have saved personal fortunes.

It has meant some of the richest people in the UK collected more than £1 million each in capital gains in 1 year by exploiting a loophole which allowed them to pay tax at a rate as low as 10 percent rather than the much higher 45 percent.

Most prominent in this practice are private equity fund managers who receive most of their remuneration in the form of 'carried interest', taxed as capital gains instead of income. Other highly paid professionals can convert their income into gains by retaining profits inside their companies as they approach retirement.

But of course the most flagrant examples of tax shirking are the mega social media and tech companies. Corporations including Apple, Facebook and Google avoid paying an estimated $500 billion a year in taxes by shifting their profits from higher-tax countries, such as the UK, France and Germany, to zero-tax or low-tax jurisdictions including Ireland, Luxembourg and Malta.[12] Yet all their employees are expected to pay tax to the country where they work and live.

Joseph E. Stiglitz, Nobel laureate in economics, professor at Columbia University and chief economist at the Roosevelt Institute, says the time has come for a minimum global corporation tax:

> Given the scale of the problem, it is clear that we need a global minimum tax to end the current race to the bottom (which benefits no one other than corporations)... A global minimum tax rate should be set at a rate comparable to the current average effective corporate tax, which is about 25 percent.

Such a universal reform would require global cooperation and would be fiercely resisted by the tech giants who have already demonstrated their opposition through obfuscation and hardball lobbying. But neither are we making it easier for ourselves. In November 2019, twelve EU countries, including Ireland, blocked a proposed new rule that would have forced multinational companies to reveal how much profit they make and how little tax they pay in each of the twenty-eight member states.[13] (Britain didn't vote because we were in the middle of a general election.) The combined vested interests of the low-taxing states and the lobbying mega-companies will be difficult to overcome, nowhere more so than in Britain, which is at the heart of a complex web of tax havens, shadow companies, financial advisers and corporate lawyers, all busy hiding wealth and avoiding tax. Transparency International, the anti-corruption organisation, has estimated that £325 billion of funds have been 'diverted by rigged procurement, bribery, embezzlement and the unlawful acquisition of state assets', from more than 100 countries – mostly in Africa, the former Soviet Union, Latin America and Asia. And in much of this shady dealing, 'you will find a UK nexus'. Transparency International's report concludes: 'This is corruption that hurts the poorest in global society, hampers progress and equality, and for which there should be no hiding place for its proceeds in the UK'.[14]

The author and fairer capitalism campaigner Nicholas Shaxson says the best way to create a level playing field of global finance is to shrink the City:

> Tax billionaires and multinationals effectively, crack down properly on all those who take crooked money from overseas, and implement radical, widespread transparency. In short, the opposite of a tax-haven strategy. Not only will this curb corruption in poorer countries, but…it will make the UK better off overall.[15]

All this seems a million miles away from people like Melanie Woolcock, whose own tax problems could not be more different from those of the City fund managers, oligarchs and tax exiles. How is changing the taxing jurisdiction for Facebook and Starbucks going to keep Melanie Woolcock out of prison? How is shrinking the City going to make the

ordinary workers better off? Will these shifts in global reg-
ulation and fiscal reform change anything for you and me?
Probably not for a very long time, even if there were the political will to make such changes in the face of such powerful
vested interests.

As we have already learned, half of Britain's land and a
quarter of its wealth is owned by just 1 percent of the population. In 2018 the wealth of the richest 1,000 people in the UK
was £724 billion, far greater than the poorest 40 percent of
households combined (£567 billion). It has increased by £274
billion in 5 years[16] and will continue to do so for as long as you
care to measure it. Because the super-rich are secretive and
protected by financial privacy laws, the spread of wealth could
well be even more restricted than these known figures suggest.

To tackle global inequality we must, of course, introduce a
more progressive income tax regime and clamp down on corruption to try to tip the scales of wealth imbalance. But if we
really want to prevent more Melanie Woolcocks from being
sent to prison and encourage Rinat Akhmetov to share some
of his wealth, drastic action is required.

The question must then turn from tackling the income
and investments of the wealthy to imposing meaningful
taxes on the transfer of wealth between generations. Under
the current law estates pay 40 percent tax on assets above
£325,000 – or above £450,000 if the family home is given
to children or grandchildren. It is a tax that has absolutely no
impact on wealth inequality in this country, allowing families
to continue to profit from handing down their untouched
fortunes to relatives.

For example, the heirs of the late sixth Duke of Westminster
paid no inheritance tax on the bulk of his £8.3 billion family

fortune following his death in 2016. Probate records show that Gerald Cavendish Grosvenor, who died aged 64 years in August 2016, left a personal estate of £616,418,184 after paying debts and liabilities. Most of this wealth had already been transferred to family trusts, carefully structured to avoid inheritance tax, which was passed on to his 28-year-old son Hugh. Hugh also inherited the title, becoming the seventh Duke of Westminster and the world's 108th richest person.[17]

The transfer of wealth at death is still the most significant means by which the top tier of wealthy families are able to maintain their status and riches. In this way social inequality is reproduced across generations so that a clutch of wealthy dynasties continue to prosper from a wealth-generating, rather than an income-generating, economy.

A fascinating study tracking rare English surnames, such as Pepys, Bigge and Nottidge, has concluded that, down the generations, the 'iron law' of inheritance has consistently trumped all efforts to improve social mobility in England and Wales. Or, as Professor Gregory Clark and Dr Neil Cummins, the two economists behind the study, explain: 'To those who have, more is given'.

After examining the records of 18,869 people, and dividing them into three categories – the rich, the prosperous and the poor – Clark and Cummins suggest that the passing on of wealth is far more persistent over the generations than previously acknowledged, noting that there is a 'significant correlation between the wealth of families five generations apart'. Put simply, the descendants of the wealthy of 1858 are still much wealthier than the average person today. The authors have rather doomily concluded that 'measures to promote social mobility have little prospect of succeeding. It's always going to be the case that families with the greatest abilities will just pass them on to their children'. These 'abilities' usually derive from nothing more than the good fortune to have been born into a wealthy and well-positioned family.

Thomas Piketty is professor of economics at the Paris School of Economics and author of the pioneering *Capital in the Twenty-First Century* and more recently *Capital and Ideology*. He has used economic data going back 250 years to show that wealth is being accumulated by a very narrow self-perpetuating cohort. He has also identified the weakness of inheritance tax laws as the principal instrument of rising wealth inequality.

If millions of ordinary people are going to have the chance of getting rich in Britain, then the government will need to embark on a radical and much more progressive taxation system for spreading more wealth across wider distributions of the population. It's not just that the current system is not fair; it also undermines capitalism, a view not restricted to hard-left politicians and their Marxist economist advisers.

As strange as it seems, there is evidence now that some of the very rich elite who benefit from these wealth-friendly taxes actually support the introduction of a tax system that would penalise them for being rich. On 24 June 2019, eighteen prominent millionaires and billionaires wrote a letter to all the US 2020 presidential candidates demanding that they bring in new laws to impose heavier taxes on the 'richest one-tenth of the 1 percent'. In other words, they were calling for the new government to tax extreme wealth. The letter called for a 'wealth tax' in order to fund climate change initiatives.

And at the height of the 2020 pandemic eighty-three millionaires, mostly Americans, signed an open letter calling on governments around the world to tax them more to help fund the economic recovery from the coronavirus crisis. Those who signed the letter said:

> The problems caused by, and revealed by, COVID-19 can't be solved with charity, no matter how generous. Government leaders must take the responsibility for raising the funds we need and spending them fairly. We can ensure we adequately fund our health systems, schools, and security through a permanent tax increase on the wealthiest people on the planet, people like us.[18]

In Britain, where we do not have the same history of philanthropic contribution, evidence of the super-rich looking for ways to redistribute their wealth is harder to find. But in 2010 JK Rowling, author of the *Harry Potter* series and whose net worth approaches $100 million,[19] set out in *The Times* newspaper her own manifesto for honest taxation in the UK:

> I chose to remain a domiciled taxpayer for a couple of reasons.[20] The main one was that I wanted my children to grow up where I grew up, to have proper roots in a culture as old and magnificent as Britain's; to be citizens, with everything that implies, of a real country, not free-floating ex-pats, living in the limbo of some tax haven and associating only with the children of similarly greedy tax exiles.

Others have gone further: Blackhall Colliery is a former pit village in County Durham. Since 2014 a few lucky residents have found bundles of £2,000 abandoned on the streets. In total £26,000 has been handed in to the police who, in turn, unable to establish its provenance, have returned it to the finder.

In January 2020 the mystery of Blackhall's discarded cash was finally solved: the benefactors told police they had received 'unexpected windfalls' and wanted to give something back. One of the Good Samaritans – who both wished to remain anonymous – said she felt an 'emotional connection' to the former pit village after being helped by a resident and wanted to 'repay the kindness she received'. If only more of the wealthy were similarly sentimental about giving back to their communities. But we can't rely on altruism and philanthropy, as even philanthropic billionaires are discovering, to transform our grossly uneven system which redistributes wealth from the workers to the lucky few. We must urge governments to act on our behalf.

10

BORN POOR

THE IMMIGRANT WHO WANTED
TO BE A SOCIAL WORKER

Maryam was born into the perfect storm.

Raised in Somalia, Maryam Ahmed's family escaped inter-clan persecution and poverty by moving to the UK in the late 1980s when she was just 3 years old. They were granted refugee status and settled in Dewsbury, Yorkshire. Her father found work in a textile factory making cheap clothes for sale to Europe and America.

Maryam attended the local comprehensive school but left early with only three GCSE passes so she could help her mother look after the house and care for her three younger brothers. Then, as soon as she was twenty-one, and her brothers were old enough to look after themselves, Maryam started searching for her first job:

> I felt ready to do something for myself, to get my independence. My parents said I shouldn't because they wanted me to marry. But I wanted to try working first. I wrote to loads of different places for jobs: a clothes factory, a fish and chip shop, a pizza place…even a garden centre. But none of them wanted me. All the time my mum and dad just kept saying that I should have listened to them.

But Maryam wasn't going to give up that easily.

I went to the job centre but they just had the same jobs I already wrote to. I asked one of the managers what she thought I should do next. Do you know what she said? 'Try changing your name…' I thought she was being funny but after a few weeks of getting nowhere with my applications I started to think it might not be a bad idea. So I did.

Maryam anglicised her first name to Maryanne and made her surname double-barrelled so she identified as Maryanne Ahmed-Smith.

Within 2 weeks I got two job interviews, one as a receptionist at a pickle factory and the other as a teaching assistant at a school. But I didn't get them. They asked loads of questions about my religion and whether I was married. I think they were put off by my niqab. In fact, the school said my clothes were too depressing for the children. It made me feel bad and I kind of lost my confidence. I thought my mum and dad were right about what they said.

But a few weeks later she got a call from the pickle factory asking her to come back for a second interview.

I decided before I went that I was going to wear my hijab [a head scarf rather than the full-face covering niqab], so they knew I was trying to get the job. After I left my house I went into the park and when no one was watching took off the niqab and put on the hijab. I felt bad because I was betraying my family and my religion, but I knew God would look into my heart and know I was doing the right thing.

When the man interviewing Maryam saw she was not wearing a full-face cover he seemed pleased and stuck out his hand to greet her.

But my faith does not let me touch men, so I had to tell him that I was Muslim and it was haraam. I touched my heart instead to show that I was pleased to meet him. His face changed and he didn't look happy with me. It was no surprise when I didn't get the job.

Eventually Maryam joined an agency and was given shifts as an office cleaner. But the work paid less than the minimum wage and because most of her shifts were at night she felt vulnerable in the building. One evening a group of young office workers had decided to have a pre-drinks party while Maryam was working. She painfully recalled:

They started making rude comments about me and one of the men tried to stop me moving into the other office. He used his body to block the door and then held me by my arm. I was really frightened and quit the agency the next day.

There was not much Maryam could have done to change her experience of the British workplace. Her job opportunities and working conditions were predetermined on the day she was born. As a black woman from Somalia she faced the triple lock of being female, BAME (black, Asian and minority ethnic) and Muslim.

Women workers in the UK are paid on average nearly 9 percent less than men. In Maryam's case cleaners can expect an even greater earning disparity of 11 percent. In part-time work the pay gap between men and women rises to 17 percent. These wide differences in overall pay have remained stubbornly high, and the ONS reports that since 2012 there has been little meaningful change in the gender pay gap. In fact, in 2019 the pay gap between men and women actually increased from the year before.[1]

For black women workers the conditions are even tougher. In 2018 UK-born black African employees were paid 7.7 percent less than UK-born white British workers with similar occupation and education characteristics. For black African workers born outside the UK, the pay gap rises to 15 percent.[2]

As a Muslim woman Maryam is part of the most economically disadvantaged and discriminated against group in the UK. Unemployment rates for Muslims are more than twice that of the general population (12.8 percent compared with 5.4 percent) and 41 percent are economically inactive, compared with 21.8 percent of the general population. The disadvantage is greater still for Muslim women: 65 percent of economically inactive Muslims are women. A 2019 House of Commons report found the reasons behind this to be varied and complex.[3] But they identified these key inhibiting factors: discrimination and Islamophobia, stereotyping, pressure from traditional families, a lack of tailored advice around higher education choices, and insufficient role models across education and employment.

The level of disadvantage is particularly acute for Muslim women. They are 71 percent more likely than white Christian women to be unemployed, even when they have the same educational level and language skills. Some Muslim women also face pressures from their own communities to leave education early and not pursue full-time careers. Those who do find full-time employment often have to overcome discrimination through negative stereotyping around dress codes and language skills.[4]

The Joseph Rowntree Foundation found that Somali women like Maryam face greater economic barriers than all ethnic minority workers living in the UK. Its research showed that Somali women have an 87 percent labour market inactivity rate compared with 65 percent for Pakistani women. This compares to 29 percent for women overall. It concluded that Muslim women's experience of the labour market was affected by 'migrant heritage, migration status, which generation they are, and whether they were born into the faith or have converted'.[5]

Maryam's work options were also restricted when the family settled in Yorkshire, where only 69 percent of women are in work. In the southwest of Britain the figure is 76 percent.[6] While the national average median household wealth stands at £286,600, this figure can vary wildly depending on where you live. Households in the southeast and London are among the wealthiest in the country (£440,000) while those in Yorkshire and Humber are worth just over £200,000, the same as they were in 2008.[7] Maryam's family's economic prospects were further worsened by the timing of their arrival in the UK during the 1980s inequality boom. Between 1985 and 1993 Britain experienced a massive rise in inequality characterised by the 'yuppie years' of rising wages, rising house prices and a stock market boom.[8] But more than anything else, being born as a woman is what has most severely affected Maryam's earning capacity and any dream she may have of getting rich.

Despite some significant progress in recent years, notably Iceland, in no country in the world have women achieved economic equality with men, and women are still more likely than men to live in poverty. This means that for a woman to get rich she must overcome hurdles that are simply not there for men.

Three out of four women in developing regions of the world are in the informal economy – where they are less likely to have employment contracts, legal rights or social protection, and are often not paid enough to escape poverty. Six hundred million women are in the most insecure and precarious forms of work. Women do at least twice as much unpaid care work, such as childcare and housework, as men – sometimes ten times as much, often on top of their paid work.[9] The global value of this work each year is estimated at $10 trillion – equivalent to one-eighth of the world's entire GDP. Women work longer days than men when paid and unpaid work is counted together. That means globally, a young woman today will work 4 years more than her male counterpart over her lifetime.[10]

There is little sign that gender equality is an achievable goal and progress on closing the gender pay gap is 'dismally slow'. The Fawcett Society estimates that at the current rate of progress it will take another 60 years to bring about parity between the sexes.[11]

Iceland is ranked as the nation closest to achieving gender parity, having closed 88 percent of its gender gap, followed by Norway (84.2 percent), Finland (83.2 percent) and Sweden (82 percent). The UK in 2019 scored 76.7 percent, a slight fall compared with 2018. Most other industrialised Western nations improved their performance over the same time frame. Spain jumped from twenty-ninth place to eighth. The World Economic Forum has placed the UK's economic gender gap at fifty-eighth in the world, brought down by big gaps in the estimated earned income of women compared with men (where the UK ranks 102) as well as straightforward wage inequality (seventy-sixth). In the UK more than three times the number of women are in part-time roles compared with men.

But perhaps more concerning for the long term is that advances in artificial intelligence in the workplace are leaving women even further behind. The World Economic Forum found there were also 'massive inequalities in almost all of [the UK's] fastest-growing job clusters of the future', including cloud computing, engineering and artificial intelligence.

It is still true that the best way for women to increase their earning capacity is by getting an education. At 35 years of age Maryam had taken one dead-end job after another and was no nearer to finding secure employment. She decided to seek help from her local college which she approached for advice about adult learning. They suggested she take an access course at a Dewsbury adult education centre, where she opted to study English language, social care and law. After qualifying she planned to become a social worker. She was delighted to discover that the £3,100 funding for the 1-year course could be secured through a loan and that it would be cancelled if she successfully passed a university course in social care. But her joy soon turned sour when her father told her that the loan would incur interest, which under Sharia law is prohibited. Even the inflation-only interest that is paid on student loans for undergraduates and postgraduates is considered haraam (forbidden by the Koran) by some Islamic scholars. Her father said it didn't matter that the loan would be cancelled if Maryam went on to university. 'He told me that I would be committing a sin if I took the loan. But on the internet I found another opinion of Sharia law which said learning loans were not against Islam'.

Maryam also consulted a friend who said he thought she could accept the loan. When her father discovered what she had done he stopped talking to her. But Maryam persevered. Not only did she pass her three qualifications, she went on to study social work at Bradford University:

> I couldn't believe my luck. I wanted it so much and now I was studying to become a social worker. The fees were high [more than £9,000 a year] and I knew I was taking on a lot of debt but the alternative was to waste my life. I still carried on with the cleaning work to pay for food and travel. I kept living at home even though my parents weren't speaking to me. I couldn't afford to pay for accommodation as well. They [Maryam's parents] still expected me to cook for my father and brothers [two of the three brothers were living at home].

Several times while she was studying Maryam considered quitting the course. And even after finishing her degree with a 2:1 her dream of becoming a working qualified social worker still looked remote. She applied to nearby local authorities for a job but was turned down by all of them. When she spread her applications further afield she encountered cultural stereo-typing, with interviewers questioning whether as a Muslim woman she would be prepared to travel for her job. 'It was so stupid because all I wanted to do was to leave home. But they just didn't seem to believe me'.

Maryam's experience of prejudice and poorer attainment in recruitment is shared by hundreds of thousands of other Muslim women who have qualifications similar to those of their white counterparts but fail to get the same kind of jobs. The Joseph Rowntree Foundation report, Supporting Ethnic Minority Young People from Education into Work, found that highly qualified Muslims are more likely to be unable to use their skills to their advantage: 39 percent of Pakistani and Bangladeshi graduates were underemployed compared with 25 percent of their white peers.[12]

One reason for this is that Muslim students are less likely to go to Russell Group universities and instead opt to attend local universities.[13] Iman Abou Atta from Faith Matters told the House of Commons committee:

In interviews and definitely in the research that has been done around women in general, Muslim women tend to be asked more than white British women about marriage, about their childcare, about whether they are looking to have this marital status… It is definitely a difference between white British women and Muslim women.

Maryam's brothers' prospects were almost as bleak as hers. And for one of them they were terminal: her middle brother died from a drug overdose after fighting years of depression. No one has suggested that his death can be blamed on the poverty he was born into. Yet had he come into the world in a more affluent part of Britain, or been presented with better opportunities, his depression and his response to his illness might have been different.

People living in more affluent areas live significantly longer than people living in deprived areas. Just across the other side of the same street, you might find a 7-year difference in life expectancy. In London some residents of neighbouring streets might have their lives cut short by a decade. The greatest disparity is in Westminster, where the average life expectancy for people over sixty-five in Lancefield Street, Queen's Park, is 83.72 years. Less than 3 miles away in the same borough, those living in the mansions of Belgravia's Grosvenor Crescent were living 10.28 years longer (to age 94).[14]

Between 2015 and 2017 men living in the least deprived 10 percent of areas in England could expect to live 9.3 years longer than men living in the 10 percent most deprived areas, and for women the gap was 7.5 years. Much of this inequality is caused by higher mortality from heart and respiratory disease, and lung cancer, in more deprived areas. These health differentials have been cruelly exposed by the coronavirus pandemic which has proportionally claimed more lives in poorer neighbourhoods.

The gap in healthy life expectancy at birth is even greater – about 19 years for both males and females, and those living in the most deprived areas spend nearly a third of their lives in poor health, compared with only about a sixth of those in the least deprived areas.[15]

Newborn baby deaths, the starkest of all markers of life's lottery, appear to have made an unwelcome return. Infant mortality had been stable or dropping for 8 of the 10 years from 2007. But in 2015 there was an increase in newborn mortality rates for the two groups with the lowest incomes and, in 2016, infant mortality went up in four out of five income groups – all but the most affluent.[16]

In the past few years life expectancy has mysteriously slowed across Europe, but the slowdown has been greater in the UK.[17] There is enough socioeconomic evidence now to show that reduced life expectancy and lifelong hardship go hand in hand. A 2020 report by the Social Mobility Commission found that children from less well-off families in some parts of England will end up in low-paid jobs no matter how well they do at school. Such persistent poverty means that families, like Maryam's, risk being 'locked into disadvantage' for generations.[18] Life for many people born in the UK is predestined, mapped out for them along regional, cultural and economic divides that separate us into winners and losers before we've even had a chance to live.

The centrifugal forces that are sucking all the wealth and the workers with specialist skills into London and the southeast is draining the regions of their natural riches and economic lifeblood. These wide differences between urban and rural economies haven't been seen since the Industrial Revolution. Today the populations of Europe's richest cities are likely to be younger, more highly educated and wealthier than Europeans who live in less successful cities and towns. The political effects of regional sifting are ingrained frustration at relative economic decline in poorer regions, a sense of loss of community as younger people leave and grievance about metropolitan 'elites' running the country for their own benefit.

It is the rise of the services economy that has been blamed for stimulating this growing regional inequality. In a services-dominated economy, centripetal forces (which encourage capital and high-skilled labour to cluster together geographically) overwhelm centrifugal forces (capital chasing ever cheaper land and labour). The American author Bill Bishop wrote a book about population movements and political polarisation in the United States entitled *The Big Sort: Why the Clustering of Like-Minded America Is Tearing Us Apart*. He argues that Western populations are self-dividing into two separate, loose groupings: highly educated, liberal and often younger people are living together in the richer cities while less-educated, conservative and older people are increasingly moving to suburbs, smaller towns and rural areas.[19]

This is being mirrored in Europe. In the 1980s and 1990s industrial heartlands, such as the Ruhr area in Germany and the mining communities of Britain, suffered from relative – and in some cases, absolute – decline in industrial output. The largest cities and regions near them – often capitals such as Paris or London – were able to replace declining industrial production with high-value services, especially tradable services such as finance, tech, culture and advertising, and in some cases, such as Munich, also with high-tech manufacturing. But while the jobs moved, the people didn't: there aren't many former miners working in tech start-ups.

In 2019 the Centre for European Reform, a Brussels-based think tank, published a paper entitled 'The Big European Sort? The diverging fortunes of Europe's regions'. Its authors argued that both sides of the debate have paid too little attention to clustering, which is in turn stimulated by the rise of services and high-tech firms. High-value-added services and technology firms have a greater tendency to cluster closely together than manufacturing firms, which tend to spread out over space, as companies seek cheaper land and labour.

This single phenomenon has remade the whole economic landscape of the country, exaggerating the already extreme regional differences in work and life experiences.

Successful city–regions are now gobbling up graduates and young people, and this trend seems to be increasing: output in business services has become more unequal across regions since the financial crisis, and education has become more strongly associated with productivity over time. This means that Europeans are being sorted both politically and economically, as well-educated young people are less likely to vote for populist parties than older, less-educated people.

This creates a dilemma for Europe's policy-makers. Should they attempt to invest in areas in relative decline, to try to stem the outflow of highly skilled people and address the frustration of people 'left behind'? Or should they invest more in skills, housing and transport to make it easier for people to join already successful cities? While the latter might lead to the largest productivity gains, it risks hardening Europe's political fault lines.[20]

Right now we are doing nothing. The political inertia that has kept discriminated women, like Maryam, in their place for generations needs to be challenged – as does the growing life and health chances between those living in rich and poor parts of the country. If we continue to do nothing, we will leave a damaging social and political divide between ageing suburbs and restive rural areas and the all-consuming distorting wealth of the great cities.

11

BORROWERS

THE RAILWAY ENGINE MECHANIC WHO LOST HER JOB AND NEVER RECOVERED

Sarah Johnson prides herself on working for a living and being able to pay her own way. But in 2014 she lost her job as a London Underground maintenance engineer:

> They told me that I had to work at a different depot because they were changing the working rotas. I said I couldn't get back from the new office in time to pick up my daughter from school. They said they would try to find an alternative arrangement but they couldn't. So I just refused to work at the new depot. They sacked me.

Sarah, who is a single parent, says she has never recovered from the shock of losing her job:

> I didn't think they would get rid of me just like that. I went to grievance appeal and everything but was just told that the private company who employed me has the right to make people work at the depot they want them to work.

The trauma of losing a job which has become so integral to a person's self-esteem can be debilitating. It took Sarah

7 months to find another job. It was 7 months of uncosted living which left her almost £20,000 in debt. 'I took out a loan to tide me over and maxed out my credit cards. The new job was only part-time so I wasn't saving any money, nor was I paying off the loans'.

Towards the end of 2014 Sarah sought help from the government to top up her income. She was granted tax credits, child benefit, housing benefit and council tax support, together worth about £900 a month, which she added to her monthly wage of £800. But the following year she received a letter from her local authority telling her that her housing benefit was going to be reduced because she had an extra bedroom in her property that wasn't being used:

> I'd heard about the bedroom tax but I didn't think the tiny spare room I use for ironing and storage counted as a bedroom. It was a bit of a blow because I couldn't afford to make up this shortfall in my housing benefit. It was about this time that one of the credit card companies threatened to take me to court if I didn't pay off the money I owed them straight away.

Sarah advertised for a lodger to make up for the loss in housing benefit. The extra rent reduced her benefits such that overall she was only £50 a month better off. But the man who took the room turned out to be trouble. He drank excessively in the evening when he came back to the house from work and was often loud and inappropriate. Sarah once overheard him telling her 13-year-old daughter he liked the way she dressed:

I started to get anxious whenever we were both in the house and I dreaded speaking to him. I told him that I thought he should go but he said he had nowhere else and that he would change his behaviour. But he didn't. In the end we had a massive barney and we just stopped talking to each other.

Sarah's daughter persuaded her to see her general practitioner because she was worried about the effect the lodger and the growing debts were having on her mother's health. The doctor said that her earlier redundancy had been more traumatic than she realised at the time. He suspected that it had left her with a form of post-traumatic stress disorder exacerbated by the incident with the lodger. The doctor prescribed Tramadol[1] and Sertraline, common antidepressants for generalised anxiety disorder, and referred her to a psychologist for cognitive behavioural therapy. But neither treatment improved her sense of worthlessness and social anxiety.

When the Department for Work and Pensions discovered that Sarah had rented out the spare bedroom and that her income had gone up, they wrote to her saying that this constituted a change in circumstance that meant she would have to reclaim all her benefits under Universal Credit:

> I thought this would be good for me as I would have all my payments given to me together at the end of the month in one big cheque. I would be able to organise my finances better. I was told that I might even get more money.

But a first-time applicant claiming Universal Credit does not receive any benefits for the first 5 weeks:

This left me short as I went without any tax credits for an extra week and had to ask the council for more money [a discretionary housing payment]. But when the first UC cheque arrived it was bigger than I thought it was going to be. After I had worked everything out it meant I was about £90 up each month. Happy days!

Two months later, however, the DWP wrote to Sarah again to notify her that they had miscalculated her UC payment. The letter was ambiguous as it did not directly ask her to repay the money. Sarah believed that the only logical interpretation was that they were demanding repayment. This triggered a panic attack and an emergency visit to the doctors, who upped her prescription.

Her debts were rising each month even though she was paying off what she could:

It was really bugging me because it didn't seem to make any difference as to whether I paid them or not. The interest on the credit cards meant they just kept going up and now the DWP wanted money as well.

In total, excluding the DWP overpayment, Sarah's debts had reached £26,340.

In 2019 Sarah's daughter came home from school to find her mother locked in the downstairs bathroom. She had had a nervous breakdown and overdosed on antidepressants. She was still conscious and with the help of her daughter she was managed into her bed and an ambulance was called.

Sarah spent a week in hospital and was signed off work sick. Her daughter, now eighteen, was old enough to look after herself and keep an eye on her mother after she left hospital. But the bills kept coming. Sarah's daughter knew how badly her mental health had been affected by her financial problems and so didn't pass on any letters that looked like bills. She was in her final year at sixth form college studying for her A levels and so couldn't take on her mother's debts even though she desperately wanted to.

She did manage to contact the DWP to tell them that her mother was off work after suffering a mental breakdown. She was put through to her mother's 'work coach' who sympathised but insisted on seeing some evidence. Sarah emailed him a copy of the psychiatric consultant's letter, which detailed her latest 'episode'. But at a meeting at the job centre with the 'work coach' she was assessed to be 'fit for work'. Sarah was warned that if she didn't start actively looking for work she would be 'sanctioned' – have her benefits docked. She returned to the house more distressed than ever.

In August 2019 a debt collector from an agency representing a credit card company visited Sarah's home. He told her that because the company had not received a reply to their final demand letters, a court order had been approved for the recovery of £2,579. She could pay it now or the bailiff would start seizing her property. She should expect him in the next few days. Sarah asked him to give her a few days to put her affairs in order.

Later that afternoon Sarah took another overdose.

★★★

There are laws in place to help people struggling with mental health and debt. One in four of us will have a mental health problem at some point in our lives. One in two adults with debts suffers from mental health issues.[2] Sarah could have written to the credit card company and her other debtors asking them to write off her debt because of the serious nature of her mental health. The financial industry recognises the problem and will waive debt in some serious circumstances. Sarah may have only needed to fill out a debt-and-mental-health evidence certificate and have it signed by a doctor. At the very least she might have reduced the interest payments and prevented court action being taken against her.[3]

But for many people suffering from mental health problems this presents a catch-22 situation: you have to be pretty lucid in the first place to write a letter to a bank or credit card company requesting reconsideration of their debt on grounds of ill health. And not all doctors understand the link between debt and mental health. Some doctors even charge patients £100 just to complete the form.[4]

Sarah's case is illustrative of another societal ill: the growing link between financial hardship, debt, depression and opioid abuse. Opioid prescriptions more than doubled in the UK between 1998 and 2018. This has been referred to as an opioid epidemic similar to, but not at the same scale as, the opioid crisis ravaging America.[5] Research has shown how opioid over-prescription is more acute in areas of low unemployment.[6] Britain's opioid and debt epidemics have wrought social destruction on some of the most deprived parts of the country. Some citizens are paying the highest price of all. Deaths related to the prescribed painkiller Fentanyl, a synthetic opioid considered to be 50 times more potent than heroin, rose from eight in 2008 to 135 in 2017.[7]

In January 2019 Britain's household debt mountain reached a new peak of £428 billion, with UK homes owing an average of £15,880 to credit card firms, banks and other lenders. Each household owed nearly £1,000 more than it did 12 months previously.[8] The level of unsecured debt as a share of household income is 30.4 percent, the highest it has ever been, and is well above the £286 billion summit in 2008 before the financial crisis. Trades Union Congress general secretary Frances O'Grady warns that 'household debt is at crisis level. Years of austerity and wage stagnation has pushed millions of families deep into the red'. More worrying is that about 8.3 million people in debt in the UK are unable to pay off loans or household bills.[9] Over half of all British households have unsecured debt, most commonly in the form of credit card debt (60 percent), overdraft (28 percent), personal loans (25 percent) and car finance (25 percent).[10]

For many the debts have become so overwhelming that the only way out is bankruptcy. The year 2019 saw personal insolvency numbers climb to levels not seen since the 2008 credit crunch. In 2019 there were 122,181 personal insolvencies, the highest annual total since 2010, according to figures from the government's Insolvency Service.[11] The rise was largely driven by a 9.8 percent increase in individual voluntary arrangements (IVAs) to 77,982, the highest annual figures for IVAs recorded since their introduction in 1987.

Insolvency experts blame the rise on insecure employment, delayed payments under UC and Brexit uncertainty for the steep climb in the number of people going broke. But since the pandemic of 2020 pressure on personal and corporate debt has gone off the scale.

★★★

Duncan Swift, president of the insolvency and restructuring trade body R3, said the pre-lockdown figures provided 'a worrying insight into the state of personal finances and further evidence that the economic and political turbulence of the last 12 months has taken its toll on businesses'. He said persistently low wage rises had left consumer finances vulnerable to small shocks: 'Although real wages have hit a recent high, they are still lower than they were before the financial crisis. Unemployment may be historically low but it's not necessarily secure for everyone'.[12]

The seizure of the economy in the wake of the coronavirus outbreak pushed more families to the brink, forcing them to take on debt they could ill afford.

For the poorest of families a Debt Relief Order, sometimes called a 'poor person's bankruptcy', is the only option. Since 2009 when the first orders were made, 254,000 people have cancelled debts worth £2.3 billion. These orders cost £90 to secure, only apply to debts of less than £20,000 and remain on your credit history for 6 years. It's easy to take the lifeline, but people who go down this route don't get rich.

Those who are already rich, of course, are subject to different debt laws.

Debt is only a problem if you have to pay the money back. I know of one entrepreneur who had thirty-three credit cards and debts of £330,000 but was still able to keep his Maserati and Ferrari on the road and continue sending his kids to private schools. He was broke but never seemed to be hard-up. There are many clever ways to stay afloat in this way. Recently, for instance, concerns have been raised about the growth in the use of a business debt-dodging trick known as 'phoenixing' where directors avoid debts by dissolving a company then start up a near-identical business with a new name.[13]

Even rich people go bankrupt sometimes. So why is it that they never seem to actually run out of money? The discredited businessman Dominic Chappell was made bankrupt three times but he was still able to buy the high street chain BHS for £1 in 2015 from the disgraced high street retailer Philip Green. The following year the company collapsed with the loss of 11,000 jobs. When the deal went sour, Chappell was eventually found guilty of three charges of neglecting or refusing to provide information and documents to the pensions regulator. He was ordered to pay a fine of £50,000 and £37,000 court costs. Incredibly, Chappell was allowed to argue that he could not pay because he had 'no funds'. He cited extensive and expensive outgoings of almost £9,000 per month made up of: £3,800 a month rent on a Dorset mansion; £2,666 a month leasing on a 2017 Range Rover; and £2,500 a month in school fees for his two children, aged 8 and 12 years, on which he was in arrears. It wasn't until 2019 that he was finally banned from being a company director.

The collapse of BHS was the biggest high street failure since the 2008 financial crisis and left a £571 million pensions black hole. Philip Green, who owned BHS for 15 years, agreed to hand over £363 million to the BHS pension scheme but escaped without a ban and also kept his knighthood. He remains a very rich man. Frank Field, the MP who chaired Parliament's Work and Pensions Committee that investigated Green and Chappell's role in the BHS collapse, said: 'Here's yet another example of the monkey being shot while the organ grinder goes free'.

Similarly, the former Wimbledon tennis champion Boris Becker was bankrupt in 2017, owing millions to various creditors. He was so broke that he said he was forced to put his treasured tennis memorabilia up for sale to settle his debts. But he didn't let his impoverished circumstances affect his luxurious lifestyle: in 2019 he was reported to be living in a £5 million riverside penthouse and driving a £60,000 car.

On a much more extreme scale, Donald Trump may have never personally filed for bankruptcy, but his companies have gone bankrupt six times. The first time was in 1991, with the Trump Taj Mahal casino in Atlantic City. Then several more of his casinos and hotels went bust in 1992. It happened again in 2004 and 2009.

'I've cut debt – by the way, this isn't me personally, it's a company', Trump said, according to *Forbes*. 'Basically I've used the laws of the country to my advantage…just as many, many others on top of the business world have'. According to the *New York Times*, he paid no federal income tax in 10 of the 15 years from 2000 to 2015. And that was before he had a hand in *making* those laws.

To understand the difference between the rich and the poor bankrupt, it's important to recognise why the banks and private equity investors treat rich bankrupts differently. To qualify for this special treatment, the bankrupt needs to have had wealth in which high-rolling investors retain an ongoing financial stake. This kind of debt is attractive because it still retains a value that can be bought, sold and gambled. And by taking advantage of complex financial credit schemes, a rich bankrupt need never be 'broke'. In sharp and tragic contrast, the payday-loan industry and high-interest credit plans that cater to the poorer end of the market drive people into deeper poverty. There are lots of poor people, and when inevitably one of them reaches the end of their tether, they are simply written off as one of many high-risk, high-yield investments.

The very wealthy have always taken their lead on responsible budgeting from politicians, who rarely let debt dictate the viability of their policies or hold back their personal ambitions. Every single recent big-budget government project, whether it is HS2, Crossrail, nuclear power stations, aircraft carriers or a new NHS hospital, has run into serious overspend. The fairer-tax campaign group, Taxpayers' Alliance, calculated in 2019 that ten of the UK's major government projects have overruns that have grown to a total of 32.7 years and £17.2 billion, or £624 per UK household.[14]

Before the coronavirus pandemic struck, Britain's national debt stood at £1.8 trillion[15] and has more than trebled since 2006. In 2019 it represented 84.2 percent of the gross domestic product (GDP), 24.2 percentage points above the EU guidelines. We might no longer have to follow those guidelines, but Britain first exceeded that figure in March 2010 when debt was 69.1 percent of the GDP. (In 2001, for comparison, it was 30 percent.) The problem is that the deficit between state spending and state income continues to drive up the national debt each year. In 2019 it was increasing at a rate of £30 billion every year as successive governments failed to balance the books. During the partial shutdown of the economy in 2020 the Treasury took on additional spending that has pushed the national debt beyond £2 trillion – the highest in our history.[16]

Since 1990 the UK economy has found sufficient bandwidth to waste trillions of pounds on foreign misadventures and financial catastrophe. Yet the economy has continued on its inexorable growth trajectory. To the ordinary worker, who is trying to make ends meet, it is hard to understand how the Treasury had so much money to spend in the first place and even harder to rationalise where it has gone. And this was before the world economy went into a post–virus meltdown and governments ripped up the rules on fiscal budgeting.

World debt – whether corporate debt, household debt or national debt, whether in developed or developing economies – is a virus on the global economy. The World Bank, in a long-view report, has shown how the global economy has experienced four waves of broad-based debt accumulation since 1970.[17] In the latest wave, under way since 2010, global debt grew to an all-time high of 230 percent of the world's GDP in 2018. The debt build-up was particularly fast in emerging market and developing economies. Since 2010 total debt in these economies has risen by 54 percentage points of the GDP to a historic peak of about 170 percent of the GDP in 2018. Following a steep fall during 2000–10, debt has also risen in low-income countries to 67 percent of the GDP ($268 billion) in 2018, up from 48 percent of the GDP (around $137 billion) in 2010.

This debt growth, warns the World Bank, is particularly worrying for emerging markets which hold about $50 trillion in debt, rendering them particularly vulnerable to any shock, whether an international recession, more trade wars or another pandemic. Developing countries have already been through three debt crises – in the 1980s, the 1990s and the 2000s – with hugely painful consequences. A fourth crisis might be on the way, the World Bank says, with similarly damaging consequences to the world economy: 'The fourth wave looks more worrisome than the previous episodes in terms of the size, speed, and reach of debt accumulation'.

The sheer amount of global debt means that any financial market correction would have immediate impact, especially on countries with few built-in economic shock absorbers.

Even advanced economies such as the UK are potentially vulnerable, with a heavily indebted corporate sector. If corporate defaults rise, which could lead overvalued stock markets to plummet, that would have knock-on effects on consumer sentiment, which in turn would have a huge impact on UK growth expectations.[18]

When challenged on our debt crisis, politicians now argue that it doesn't matter because we can pay it off ourselves by printing more money. But this fails to understand that monetary and fiscal recklessness devalues the pound, damages trade and drives up inflation. Nor does it explain why the government didn't use the same argument to spend our way out of recession rather than go down the austerity road. Nor does it account for Westminster's troubling insouciance concerning the whereabouts of £50 billion of printed banknotes which the National Audit Office says have simply disappeared into a 'shadow economy' used by tax exiles and money launderers.[19] The truth is national and global debt is treated as an inconvenience that need not prevent governments from doing what they want to do.

The US and its allies spent $3 trillion on the war in Iraq and another $3 trillion on the war in Afghanistan. Wars which the West lost. The Ministry of Defence estimates the UK alone spent £20 billion on both conflicts. Before that, when Britain crashed out of the European Exchange Rate Mechanism, the national coffers took a hit of £4 billion. The credit-crunch crisis of 2008 cost the British economy £7 trillion and the Treasury responded by pumping in £500 billion to rescue the banks. Estimates for the cost to the British economy of Brexit start at £40 billion and go beyond £200 billion, though no one really knows what the final bill will be.

In the end it doesn't matter. If the government runs out of money it will print more. If the rich go bankrupt they can shuffle things around so that they can keep hold of their luxury homes and sports cars. Still, one can easily imagine how the conversation might have run if Sarah Johnson, the person who lost her job as a London Underground maintenance engineer, had informed her 'work coach' that she was taking out a loan that she had no intention of repaying.

12

STRIVERS

THE £90,000 LAWYER WHO DIDN'T FEEL VERY RICH

John Burghard thought he had made it. After 4 years of studying law and another 10 years working in a City legal practice, John was looking forward to a very comfortable, middle-class middle age. With a guaranteed salary of £90,000 plus generous bonuses, he and his wife could finally live out their dreams. They bought a modest stone-built, period home, nestled in the picturesque Cotswolds. Their neighbours were Jeremy Clarkson and David Cameron. Holidays were of the exotic rather than the package type, and their kids were safely ensconced in private schools.

But today John and his wife Sarah aren't feeling quite so flush. With one salary, cancelled bonuses, no savings and 'hundreds of thousands of pounds' owed on their twice re-mortgaged home, the family finances are not looking very rosy at all.

'I know it sounds ridiculous but we are finding it very difficult', worries John, who says the cost of supporting the family's Cotswold lifestyle has become impossible.

John has always thought of himself as well off, maybe not as rich as some of his law school mates who got jobs at the 'Magic Circle' firms in the City, but on a big enough salary to pay for everything he needs and still have a work/life balance.

> Of course there are weeks when we are really under the cosh and we have to get a deal over the line. Then I'll probably stay in town until the worst of it's over. But most of the year I can pretty much guarantee I'm out of the door by 6pm and home with Sarah and the kids from 8:30pm. I know I'm not earning top dollar – but that's the trade-off.

But recently John has come to the realisation that neither his work-life commitments nor his family budgets are balancing. Because John works in London, his standard rail season ticket between Moreton-in-Marsh and Paddington and parking at the station costs £7,500 a year. Even at that price it doesn't guarantee John a seat, so if he is busy at work, in the middle of a deal and needs to prepare documents and send emails, he has no choice but to book a first-class ticket:

> It is either that or standing up with all the other penguins for half the journey trying to work on my iPhone. I'm so stressed by the time I get to work that it takes me an hour to calm down before I'm working efficiently again in the office.

On top of the rail fares, John also has an Oyster card to pay for the Underground from Paddington to Bank. That pushes his annual travel costs to well over £10,500. As the expenses and household bills mount it is easy to see why £90,000 isn't nearly enough to support the Burghards' lifestyle.

The first thing John and Sarah have decided to sacrifice is their children's education. Sending their eldest to a state sixth form has saved them £30,000, giving them 2 years of respite before they begin paying university fees and living expenses. But their youngest son still attends an independent school in the North Cotswolds, where fees are £15,000 a year. John and Sarah recently had a meeting with the headmaster and bursar when they explained their financial predicament. John recalled the meeting as follows:

> It was somewhat embarrassing but the school was excellent. The head said that provided we paid some of the fees we could keep our son at the school. He even said there might be bursaries that would help with the fees. When I said I didn't think people like us could get a bursary or help with fees he said that there were parents on even higher salaries than me who qualified for help.

The family's other big spend was the £500,000 mortgage, which was being repaid at £1,100 a month. 'We just can't afford it so we wrote to the mortgage company requesting a "holiday" from the repayments', says John.

It isn't only the school fees and mortgage payments which John and Sarah have cut back on: dining out is reserved for special occasions and villa and pool holidays, usually taken in the Caribbean, have been exchanged for camping holidays in the South of France. Yet the debts keep mounting. 'Our margins were still very tight. The essentials, including food, and running two cars were tipping us into the red. We keep asking ourselves how did we suddenly become poor?'

The huge outgoings and equally sizeable expectations of the middle classes are leaving many struggling to stock the fridge with groceries from Waitrose each week. A £90,000 salary no longer guarantees a comfortable lifestyle. In fact, John and Sarah's story is far from unusual. They are members of a new social class, the 'squeezed middle', a high-achieving, well-paid professional class who have become overextended.

The term, coined by Oxford professor Danny Dorling,[1] refers to high earners who find themselves struggling to keep up with those raking in even bigger salaries. Although the Burghards' income is three times the national average, their lifestyle is still unsustainable. The hard-working middle classes may earn more money than those struggling at the fringes of society, but they often have no more disposable income although they may enjoy more living and recreational space. To those surviving at the lower end of the socioeconomic pile who don't have the 'headache' of worrying how to run a family on a £90,000 salary, the middle classes are simply living beyond their means. But being well off in Britain has become a very relative term.

Dorling says that a couple with two children need to earn £200,000 to scrape into the top 1 percent of well-off families. Even then you won't be considered rich. The average earnings for the top 1 percent bracket is £369,000. Further down the pay pile, the squeezed upper middle includes senior managers, lawyers, accountants, BBC executives, hospital consultants and university vice chancellors. To be in this group a single person has to earn at least £100,000, a childless couple £160,000 and a couple with two children £200,000. By this measurement it is easy to see why John and Sarah might be struggling despite having an ostensibly comfortable income.

In 2014 a government minister who was on a salary of £90,000 hit the headlines when he resigned protesting he could no longer afford to care for his family and do his job. Mark Simmonds, a minister in the Foreign Office, said that he didn't have enough money to move his three children to London from Lincolnshire. Yet the Simmonds were better off than most as Simmonds' wife was paid between £20,000 and £25,000 to be her husband's office manager and he also received around £60,000 from other non-parliamentary jobs.[2]

At the time, Sir Alistair Graham, the former chairman of the Committee on Standards in Public Life, told the BBC that he thought the public would be 'shocked to hear somebody say they couldn't manage on £90,000 a year'.[3] But few people were. The price of a home in central London has skyrocketed, making it unattainable to even some of the city's highest earners.

When Simmonds' story was reported in the media it chimed with lots of other high-paid 'strugglers'. One professional from Preston wrote:

Me and my wife jointly earn £120K a year yet we haven't had a holiday for 5 years. Struggle to pay for trips for our son. (One to the US I've had to say no to.) Can't afford to fix the cladding at the front of the house and haven't changed cars for 10 years and we live in Preston, Lancashire. How you plebs manage is beyond me.

Lisa from London added:

I work damn hard, and whilst my husband and I aren't quite in the top 1 percent, we share a six figure salary between us (no children). We've managed to buy a 3 bed semi in a nice area of greater London that needs total renovation and we're still looking at £2.6k mortgage a month. I drive a small car, I shop in Lidl and our luxuries are dinner out maybe once a week and a great holiday each year.[4]

None of this is going to garner much sympathy from those who have never had a car or a garden or even given a thought to complaining about not being able to afford to eat out or go on holiday.

Even so, the problem facing the hard-up high-earning middle classes is much more serious than a year without a holiday. Research by the Organisation for Economic Co-operation and Development (OECD) has found that more than one-third of middle-income households in the UK have difficulty making ends meet.[5] It begs the question: if those who are comfortably off are struggling too, then whom does the current economic system serve?

★★★

Across the Western world, incomes of middle-class families are stagnating as they are squeezed by the ultra-rich taking an increasingly bigger slice of the pie. Today even a family just inside the top tenth of the income distribution would have to save for 50 years to break into the top 10 percent of the wealth distribution, making it unrealistic for even the highest-paid group to accumulate large amounts of wealth without unearned independent windfalls.[6]

The truth is that every generation since the baby boom has seen the middle-income group shrink and its economic influence weaken.

The cost of essential parts of the middle-class lifestyle, particularly housing, has risen faster than income. Middle-class families can also sense that their contribution to the economy through taxes and productivity is not being reflected in their pay packets. Many have been caught by what is referred to as 'fiscal drag', where the impact of wage rises is being diluted by higher taxes. In Scotland, where research into fiscal drag has been conducted, a third more Scots have become liable for higher tax rates.[7] In 2016–17, around 307,300 Scots paid the highest tax rate, which then began at £43,000 a year, or the additional rate of 45p for those earning £150,000 per annum. But after three freezes and one below-inflation rise in the taxation thresholds, around 403,900 middle earners are now forecast to be caught by higher rates in 2020–21. This phenomenon is replicated across the UK such that the more middle earners earn, the more they are losing in taxes.[8]

The OECD has found that:

Traditional middle-class opportunities for social mobility have also withered as labour market prospects become increasingly uncertain: one in six middle-income workers are in jobs that are at high risk of automation. Uncertain of their own prospects, the middle class are also concerned about those of their children; the current generation is one of the most educated ever, and yet has lower chances of achieving the same standard of living as its parents.[9]

And the prospects of the middle-class earners are going to get worse.

The professional services economy is upskilling to artificial intelligence platforms which will cut a swathe through the middle classes, leaving an even smaller rich elite to take a select number of once safe jobs in law, insurance, accounting, engineering and even medicine.[10] There will be many people, some of whom we have already encountered in earlier chapters, who question why we should care that the middle classes are coming under financial pressure and finding it difficult to get rich. If not for ourselves, we should care because the middle class is the engine of capitalism.

The 'middle class' has always been what the vast majority of us aspire to. For many generations it meant a well-paid job, the assurance of being able to afford a house with a spare bedroom and a comfortable lifestyle with everything short of a super-yacht within reach. Perhaps more importantly, families who already called themselves middle class have always pinned their hopes and dreams on their children moving further up the economic ladder. For more than a century the presence of a strong and prosperous middle class has been the bedrock of a thriving economy and healthy societies.

Just consider the structure of global economic demand, of which private household consumption accounts for about half (the other half is evenly split between investment and government consumption). Two-thirds of this household consumption comes from the middle class. The rich may spend more per person but are too few in number to drive the global economy. The poor are numerous but have too little income to spend.[11] By contrast, more than half the world is judged to be middle class. That is 3.6 billion people who have sufficient money to cover basic needs such as food, clothing and shelter, and still have enough left over for the odd luxury such as a television, a motorbike or home improvements.

The OECD says that through their consumption, along with investment in education, health and housing, the middle classes underpin the demand for high-quality public services. Their intolerance of corruption and their trust in democratic institutions also make them the financial guardians of an economy which ensures 'inclusive growth'. Societies with a strong middle class have lower crime rates and enjoy higher levels of trust and life satisfaction, as well as greater political stability and good governance. But the OECD warns that 'there are now signs that this bedrock of our democracies and economic growth is not as stable as in the past'. The middle classes may be the dominant class but they are all competing for the same material possessions and lifestyles, preventing each other from breaking into the upper wealth class.

These aspirant lifestyles of the super-wealthy are simply unaffordable. The gap between middle-class wealth and the super-riches of the elites has become so distant that doctors, lawyers and entrepreneurs have resigned themselves to more realistic financial success. The work is just as hard but the rewards are diminished, spreading dissatisfaction among the once contented lives of the bourgeoisie who are having to come to terms with a country getting richer while its middle classes grow poorer.

13

SAVERS

THE SAILOR AND THE DINNER LADY WHO RAN OUT OF MONEY BEFORE THEY DIED

The deal between the state and the pensioner has always been transparently fair and straightforward: if you pay your taxes until you reach sixty-five the government will financially provide for your retirement.

That was the basis upon which Jack and Cynthia Queen conducted and managed most of their lives. So when Jack turned sixty and started to look forward to a new chapter in his life, it was reassuring to know that he had taken care of his future by playing by the rules and doing the right thing. Jack was part of the generation who were too young to go to war but old enough to be required to give up 2 years of their life in the national service of their country. He had family members who had made terrible sacrifices in the war and so Jack was proud to be able to play his part in the national call of duty in 1949.

After initial training Jack became a qualified 'batsman' on board the aircraft carrier HMS *Implacable* using his 'paddles' to guide Seafire fighter planes on and off the ship. He stayed in service for an extra year so that there was no doubt he had done his bit.

In 1952 he left the Navy and joined Chelmsford local authority as a town planner, rising to deputy head of planning. It was a secure job that allowed him to map out a good career:

> My older brother was killed in the war flying bombers over Germany. All I really wanted was a steady, rewarding career, a professional one if possible, that gave me a sense of purpose. I wanted to work hard but I also wanted to have time to appreciate the years of my life that my brother didn't have.

Jack married Cynthia in 1961 and they had two children. Cynthia was a full-time mum and housewife and Jack looked after all the financial matters. It was an arrangement that worked very well for them until the children left home. Then Cynthia wanted a bit of independence and got a job as a dinner lady at their children's old school. She became a union activist and fought for equal pay for the dinner ladies so that they were on a par with the caretakers and teaching assistants.

After decades of hard word, Jack and Cynthia retired in the same year, 1995, when they were sixty-five and sixty, respectively, then the national retirement ages for men and women.

'We were looking forward to a long and peaceful retirement. I had lots of plans for designing a new garden and doing some part-time planning work from the garage', remembers Jack. 'I wanted to travel the world', says Cynthia. Their retirement has indeed been long – they are both in their nineties – but it has hardly been peaceful.

Jack had saved a few thousand pounds, which he had invested in a low-risk portfolio of FTSE 100 shares. In years gone by he would have left it in the bank but the banks were 'offering' zero interest rates. They had paid off the mortgage on their three-bedroom terraced house in Mersea, close to Colchester. But neither of them had ever thought about taking out a private pension. Jack recalled:

> We had faith in the state pension. And to be honest neither of us thought we were going to live this long. When I retired I really did think we were rich. We didn't have to pay the TV licence and we had free travel with our bus pass, even the cinema and the hairdresser were subsidised. The shares were bringing in a couple of thousand pounds a year, which we used to supplement both our pensions. For a few years we did feel pretty rich, rich in the sense we had all that we really needed. Cynthia may not have travelled as far or as often as she would have liked and my part-time consultancy work never took off, but we were basically well off.

Then a series of personal catastrophes turned their life on its head. Their daughter Melanie divorced her husband and took the children with her. She left without any savings or a job and moved in with Jack and Cynthia. It was only supposed to be a stopgap for the first few months but she never seemed to be able to get back on her feet and the children were now happily settled into their new school in Colchester. It became a permanent arrangement. Soon Jack and Cynthia found that the interest on their savings and their combined pensions weren't covering the costs for all five of them. Their daughter tried to get work but in the end gave up and fell back on benefits. Jack and Cynthia thought she was just low on confidence but she was in fact suffering from severe anxiety and depression. She was diagnosed with fibromyalgia, which causes chronic pain and tiredness as well as cognitive disruption.

The extra food bill and costs of the children started to build up. The interest on the savings wasn't even coming close to covering the extra family expenses. After 2 years they had spent all their savings and had nothing to fall back on. 'We were faced with the only option', said Jack, 'and that was selling our home and taking the profit to spend on our daughter and grandchildren'. Their first thought was to downsize but they quickly realised that they still needed a three-bedroom home to accommodate the grandchildren. Instead they did what a growing number of pensioners are being forced to do in order to fund their retirement: they took out an equity-release policy on their home. Jack and Cynthia had fully paid off the mortgage a few years before they retired, so there was close to £400,000 equity in the home. 'We were probably going to leave the house to our daughter when we died', reasoned Cynthia, 'so we thought it was better to make use of the money now when she and the boys really needed it'.

Under the terms of their lifetime equity-release policy Jack and Cynthia did not have to pay a single penny of interest on the loan. Instead it was rolled up through the length of the policy (it expired when both of them died) and added to the cost of the debt. They decided to release an initial £100,000, but because of the high compound interest they soon realised that what they owed would be double that by the time they died. That wasn't a real concern to them because they couldn't live long enough to be deprived of the value of their only asset. But it did mean that any inheritance they might have wanted to pass on to their daughter and grandchildren would be severely reduced.

★★★

The first pensions have their origins in Islamic societies. Taxes collected under the seventh-century Rashidun Caliphate as a form of *zakat* (charity), one of the Five Pillars of Islam, were used to provide income for those in need which included the poor, elderly, orphans, widows and the disabled.

In England the first state pensions weren't paid out until 1908 under the Old Age Pensions Act. They were paid to people over seventy who had passed a 'good character' test. People were denied a pension if they had refused work, made themselves poor in order to qualify, had been imprisoned or were habitually inebriated. These first pensions were deliberately set at a low level that kept the recipient just above the breadline.

After the Second World War, William Beveridge's report[1] – Social Insurance and Allied Services – marked a major break with the past by introducing universal payments. But even in this apparent golden age of welfare, the objective was not to provide a high replacement income for wage earners but rather a safety net against old-age deprivation. Under Beveridge's scheme this income was to be funded through contributions paid during a person's working life.

Over time the link between a person's contributions and the pension income that person receives became weaker, and National Insurance rates are now set simply according to the overall government budget – not directly related to either future pension benefits or current pension funding needs. The state pension has certainly not been keeping up with average earnings as it was supposed to do.[2]

But in some respects OAP couples like Jack and Cynthia are the lucky ones. Many more pensioners are not fortunate enough to own their own home or able to dip into savings. Others have not had enough work to pay their National

Insurance contributions. In fact, the proportion of elderly people now living in severe poverty in the UK is five times what it was in 1986.

Since the 1980s the UK has gone from having the lowest to one of the highest rates of poverty among elderly people in western Europe.[3] Today this represents 1.6 million pensioners living in relative poverty in the UK, which is defined as not being able to afford the same things the majority of pensioners enjoy. More than half (900,000) are living in severe poverty, that is, on income of 40 percent or less of the median average. To put it more bluntly, every winter's day hundreds of thousands of pensioners must choose between a warm meal or heating the home. And those most at risk are single, non-white and living in rented accommodation.[4]

According to Professor Bernhard Ebbinghaus, of the University of Oxford, pensioners are relying on a Beveridge-lite pension system which means basic pensions are little more than sustenance allowances. Yet to be sure of even getting this, workers must have paid National Insurance for 30 full years from the age of 16 years until they retire. One in six pensioners has to supplement their state pension with a means-tested targeted benefit, which makes the UK one of the less generous basic pension systems in Europe.[5]

Which? research has found that a single person needs around £13,000 a year in retirement to cover the essentials and around £22,000 a year for a comfortable retirement. The state pension rises every year by at least 2.5 percent and in 2021 is worth about £9,400 a year. But successive governments have long encouraged pensioners to take out a private pension so that they are not forced to rely on what is now a bare-bones package of state pension and benefits later in life.

Nevertheless, many private pensions are simply too small to make any meaningful contribution to retirement. A £50,000 pension pot will purchase an annuity that pays out just £2,000 a year.[6] (To earn it back at current projected rates of inflation you'd have to live for 110 years.)

In 2015 George Osborne changed the pension rules to make it possible for anyone over 55 years of age to raid their own private pension. It meant millions of people still in work were able to take out a lump sum from their pension and spend it on whatever they liked. For many the temptation of mid-life riches was just too much to resist. The offer of 'free' cash to refurbish the kitchen or buy the dream car led to many people in their late fifties sabotaging their own retirements by reducing their pension pot and the size of the annuity to pay out later in life. The Financial Conduct Authority has warned that hundreds of thousands of middle-aged people are sleep-walking into financial disaster. They said that 100,000 private pension holders are drawing down on their own pensions without taking any kind of financial advice. Inevitably, many of them have misunderstood quite how big a nest egg they will need for a secure future.

Yet a small group can look forward to a golden retirement. The bankers and corporate executives have always retained generous pensions. And since 2010 the number of executives and managers in the public sector's largest pension schemes who are retiring on incomes of more than £100,000 has tripled.

Although the rules are now changing, the public sector has a legacy of offering very generous pensions, and these will be on the balance sheet for some time to come. In fact, despite ending final salary pensions in many cases, the public sector pension bill is still ballooning. In 2018 pension schemes covering the top earners of the NHS, the civil service and the teaching profession were paying six-figure incomes to 375 retirees, a rise of 117 on 2010. Those in receipt of pensions higher than the UK's average annual salary of around £30,000 also increased by 46 percent – up from 78,000 in 2010–11 to 115,000 in 2017–18. This means that 115,000 government pensions are now above the average annual wage.

These gold-plated public sector pensions are adding to the extreme inequality between millions of pensioners who have to get by on £9,400 a year and a lucky few who enjoy the latter parts of their lives spent in almost decadent leisure. This lopsided pension payout bonanza also has serious consequences for the generations who follow. The Intergenerational Foundation, which campaigns for a fairer deal for Britain's younger generations,[7] warns that our pension system is a major burden for younger generations who will end up working harder and longer to pay for their parents' pensions.[8] And they are doing this with the knowledge that their own pensions are going to be much less generous.

The UK population is ageing, driven by falling long-term mortality and dipping birth rates. People are living longer than ever before; infants born between 2015 and 2017 are expected to live 79.2 years if male and 82.9 years if female (an increase of 2 and 1.4 years, respectively, since 2005–2007). As life expectancy remains high, although there is evidence that it may have plateaued, birth rates continue to decrease. In 2017 there were 755,066 live births, a decrease of 2.6 percent since 2016 and the lowest number of live births since 2006. In 2017 almost one in five people in the UK were aged 65 or over compared with 15.9 percent in 1997. This percentage is expected to reach 24 percent by 2037. As you might expect, we've seen a rise in the pensions bill from £17 billion in 1989 to £92 billion in 2019, and it's going to cost £20 billion more by 2023 as the population ages.[9]

More recently governments have recognised that National Insurance contributions are unable to keep pace with our ageing population and governments, Tory and Labour, have been forced to bring in measures to raise the retirement age. Governments have already taken steps to increase the pension age to sixty-seven in 2028 and then sixty-eight by 2046, leaving us working well into our twilight years. At the same time, nearly 4 million women have already been forced to wait up to an extra 6 years to get their pensions after changes to bring women's retirement age into line with that of men.

Under Boris Johnson's administration the retirement age is expected to be raised even higher – to 70 years old, the level at which it was set in Edwardian times when the payment was handed out as a breadline pension. But how many of us will live long enough to start collecting it? In Glasgow boys born between 2015 and 2017 have a life expectancy of just 73.3 years. The rising retirement age has a discriminatory effect on people with disabilities or illness; neither does it allow for the disparity in the working life spans of a freelance bricklayer and a Whitehall pen-pusher.

Sadly, Jack and Cynthia's troubles in retirement didn't end where we left them. Cynthia had suffered a heart attack while playing club bowls with her friends in the village. She had received excellent care and treatment from the local hospital, and within days of the diagnosis she was given coronary angioplasty to open up narrowed arteries in her heart. But she now required a hip replacement operation which she had been putting off for years. Doctors said that after her heart health scare it was imperative that she lead an active life again as quickly as possible. Exercise would aid her post-op recovery and general health. Unfortunately, the next NHS hip operation wasn't available for another 9 months. Jack recalled:

> Cynthia said she was fine and that she could wait, but the doctors' advice had been very clear. I decided the best thing to do was to go private. I reckoned we still had plenty of equity left in the house so I didn't think financing it would be a problem. I got a quote from a private health company for £16,000. But when I approached the home equity company they said there was a problem because I had taken out the wrong equity-release policy.

Jack had been badly advised and should have taken out an enhanced equity-release plan which allows for drawdowns to pay for medical treatments. The company said he could have the loan but it would cost him more in interest which, although not payable until their death, ate more into the family inheritance. Frail and in their nineties they were on course to spend their last penny and still had years left to live an unknown but certainly impecunious retirement.

As more Britons grow cash-poor the equity value of their home has become a vital source of income in later life. Our ageing population means that more pensioners are living longer, outliving their modest savings and pensions. Overall £28 billion of property wealth has been borrowed by more than 487,000 people using equity release since 1991. (By the time you read this, the numbers will have already broken through half a million.) The popularity of equity-release loans has recently surged, and in 2018 a record-breaking 80,000 homeowners aged over 55 years unlocked £3.9 billion of property wealth. In 2019 a new equity-release product was launched every 2 days, and there are now more than 300 plans on the market compared with 73 plans just 3 years ago. The amount of debt can soar, wiping out the value of homes and leaving families with no inheritance. The Financial Conduct Authority has warned that the market is ripe for another mis-selling scandal akin to payment protection insurance.

But of much graver concern is the obvious comparison between the high-speed rate of take-up of these loans and the reckless sale of millions of sub-prime mortgages which triggered the credit crunch in 2008. If there were to be a property slump, or even a sharp dip, billions of pounds could be wiped off the value of the equity-release market. Companies would be forced to foreclose on their loans and the domino effect could bring about another recession. For Jack and Cynthia it would be disastrous, making them homeless and forcing them into the care of the state, not to mention their daughter and grandchildren.

One way to immediately address the pension time bomb is to bring in means testing for the state pension so that those already enjoying high-income payouts do not drain the state of funds for those genuinely in need. The Intergenerational Foundation would like to see the cut-off at those who already receive a £50,000 annual payout on their private pension. We means test other state benefits so why not pensions?

Unless something is done the problem will get worse, and it is not inconceivable that we will reach a point where the state will no longer be able to guarantee that it can support people in their twilight years.

14

TRADERS

THE DAY THE BOOKSHOP
DIDN'T SELL ANY BOOKS

Jenny Ovaltine had dreamed all her life of owning her own florists. And in 2012 her dream came true when she opened a flower shop in Basildon, Essex. She financed the purchase with a bank loan and some savings from working as a legal secretary.

There are 15,000 floristry businesses in the UK, including 8,000 physical shops and 7,000 online shops and sole traders. It's a perishable industry worth £1.5 billion, trading in a product that loses its value from the day the first flowers bud.

A few years ago the florist market started to move online and soon people were getting top quality flowers delivered to their door with all their other shopping. But Jenny didn't seem to have noticed. As it happened, when she opened her business in 2017 she couldn't have chosen a worse time to start out on the high street.

To begin with, trading was steady if not spectacular. But a combination of post-recession nervousness and competition from supermarkets and petrol stations saw a sharp drop in trade on Basildon High Road.

'Instead of a regular stream of walk-in buyers', says Jenny, 'people were shuffling past the shop in embarrassment. Stock was being wasted and in the end I couldn't *give* the flowers away'.

The bills and the creditors started mounting:

> The business rate was just stupid. I was paying hundreds of pounds a month to compete with Tesco. Soon I couldn't afford the electricity for the shop but I kept going, wearing my thermals in the winter. In the end I had to let the delivery guy go as I couldn't pay him to drop off the flowers for the customers. I ended up doing the deliveries myself at lunchtime. I was working stupid hours, always hoping that I could turn it around.

Jenny struggled for 18 months until she succumbed to the inevitable and closed the shop. By this time she had accumulated £40,000 of debt. As Jenny had no assets she decided to declare herself bankrupt.

The demise of Jenny's business is a reflection of the wider decline of the high street. Take bookshops. In January 2020 the owner of Petersfield Bookshop in Hampshire reported that for the first time in the store's 100-year history the shop had gone through a whole day without making a single sale. When this historic moment reached social media the public's reaction was extraordinary: physical and online orders went through the roof. The owner, John Westwood, said at the time:

> It has been overwhelming, mind-blowing and very humbling. Book lovers are a very special people, and everyone has been so supportive. I've carried on this store for my father – if you want to be rich you don't go into the book industry. Books

are special things and nothing beats going into a bookstore. Seeing them, touching them, smelling them – it is a special place.

I believe in this industry, but online ordering and Amazon has hit us hard. I've had to sell my flat to keep the store afloat, and most evenings I sleep on a camp bed in the shop. We have lots of big plans for the future, on how to expand and grow, we just need to survive these difficult times first.

In 2005 there were 1,535 independent bookstores in the UK. By 2020 that number had dwindled to 890 shops. Part of the challenge for the bookshop industry is adapting to the competition from e-books and online retailers, and the rising popularity of other entertainment forms such as Netflix and gaming. But the greatest impediment to a profitable bookshop is the government or, more specifically, the business rates *set* by the government.

'It's not easy', says John, 'being on the high street these days, let alone running a second-hand bookshop'. And he reserves special criticism for the 'horrendous effects' that high business rates are having on all local traders, not just his bookshop.[1] (Because business rates are measured according to floor space, bookshops are particularly vulnerable to *unfair* business rates.) John continues:

There's not even 200 [traders] now and most of the people who run them are going to retire soon, I imagine. But we're not going to give in. My dad started this business in 1958 and was renowned throughout the world for his bookselling.

★★★

All is not lost though as high street bookshops have started to make a gentle comeback. The year 2020 was the third successive year that the independent bookshop industry reported more shops opening than closing. But that is no thanks to the government. In Bedford town centre Waterstones is still paying 16 times more business tax than Amazon's nearby warehouse.[2] And we are certainly not out of the woods. A switch to online shopping and higher and higher business rates have seen thousands of shop and business closures since the 2008 credit crunch. Boxing Day 2019 witnessed the biggest decline in footfall since 2010. That year was the first since records began that retail trading actually fell, according to the British Retail Consortium (BRC).[3] This is worrying because the population increases in size every year and so figures relating to the clothing and feeding of the population should be going up on their own. Even at the height of the financial crisis or when austerity was biting hard, retail growth was nearly 2 percent.

Between 2013 and 2019 almost one out of ten high street shops in English and Welsh town centres were permanently closed. In towns such as Stoke and Blackpool the figure rises to one in five. On a broader scale, high-profile retailers are being washed away by the same anti-business conditions that are stalking the high street. In 2019 Thomas Cook, Mothercare and Debenhams collapsed into administration, contributing to hundreds of store closures and thousands of job losses in the sector.[4] Neither is the high street stalwart, the Italian or Greek restaurant, any longer a safe bet. Between 2017 and 2019 the top 100 restaurants went from raking in profits of £345 million to losses of £93 million.[5] And the number of UK hotel insolvencies hit a 5-year high in 2019 following a drop in business travel and tougher competition from Airbnb.

Not even the growing popularity of the post-Brexit staycation could reverse their fortunes. But when the pandemic swept through our high streets in 2020 the economic devastation was unprecedented, sending more well-known businesses to the wall – and many more that were hardly known at all.

We have seen how pre-COVID-19 the government took an extraordinarily laissez-faire approach to challenges confronting commerce in the community. But the banks have been even worse: self-employed entrepreneurs used to be able to rely on their high street bank for help when they were starting out or charting a course through choppy economic waters. The district bank manager knew his or her high street businesses, built up strong relationships with clients and was there to extend a lifeline loan or sage advice in rocky times. But the Royal Bank of Scotland scandal, in which banking executives forced small businesses into bankruptcy to line their own pockets or meet corporate targets, shows how far the banks have strayed from their communities in the name of 'shareholder value'.

The failure of the banks to support small businesses in the coronavirus-hit economy is equally scandalous. These are the same banks who were bailed out by the government during the last financial crisis but won't risk a little of their capital to help save the high street from economic catastrophe.

Economists believe the decline in physical retail trading could be indicative of something much more fundamental than the nation's shopping habits. If these figures related to our steel industry or car manufacturing there would be emergency questions in Parliament, trade sanctions would be threatened and Polly Toynbee in the *Guardian* would be blaming it on Brexit. Because it's easy to forget that these are not just little luxuries – people's livelihoods are at stake. The retail sector employs nearly 3 million,[6] a third of a million more than manufacturing, yet the loss of a few hundred industrial jobs is cause for national mourning while the death of the high street is being written off as inevitable. The economic ravages of the pandemic have piled on even more misery, pushing marginally profitable businesses over the edge.

We were once a nation of shopkeepers, restaurateurs and hoteliers. Opening a small business on the high street used to be a recognised step towards wealth and standing. But starting a business is no longer making people rich. Here we confront another of Britain's twenty-first-century economic paradoxes.

In recent years self-employment has actually accounted for a growing share of the national work force, rising from 12 percent of workers in 2001 to 15 percent in 2018. However, these newly created businesses aren't shopkeepers or clog-makers. These are the workers of the gig economy, the delivery and taxi drivers, the warehouse workers and the freelance office clerks – all kept off the permanent payroll and rescheduled as 'self-employed'. Most of them are underpaid. Two million people who are self-employed today receive less than the living wage,[7] making them much worse off than those in full-time employment. In 2016–17 they earned on average (by modal income) £12,300, compared with £21,600 for those in salaried jobs.[8] Sham forms of self-employment are used by giant digitalised businesses to reduce tax liability, duck the minimum wage and deny workers their rights. And when these self-employed strugglers finally admit defeat and fall on the mercy of the state they face further discrimination: under Universal Credit rules their benefits are cut because the government automatically assumes their 'businesses' are earning them a minimum wage even when they may be earning nothing at all. The Institute for Fiscal Studies worked out that as many as 450,000 low-income households see their payments cut by an average of £3,200 a year thanks to this policy, known as the 'minimum income floor'.

The founding principle of capitalism was that everyone has the same chance to get rich. The ingredients were hard work, creativity and perseverance. Entrepreneurs who set out on their own and worked their socks off would reasonably expect to make lots of money. Sam Zell, founder of Equity Group Investments, echoed the view of many wealthy entrepreneurs when he famously declared in 2012: 'The world is not a zero-sum game. If I succeed, it doesn't mean that you don't. I succeed because I am driven and I take the risks. Deal with it'.

Versions of this statement are used by all sorts of successful people to justify their riches. But we can now see this may not be true. Jenny and John are no different from any other hard-working entrepreneurs and Basildon and Petersfield are no different to any other high streets in Britain. To make it in self-employed business, it's not enough to be hard-working, creative and perseverant. To make a success of your business you must have that other vital ingredient: luck.

The fact is that the vast majority of entrepreneurs, like Jenny, are never going to realise their dreams no matter how hard they work. Yet lifestyle surveys, wealth reports and self-help business books pump out data laced with anecdotes that claim that the doorway to riches is wide open. Authors of the *Sunday Times* rich list often make out that the wealth tables increasingly comprise self-made entrepreneurs who built their fortunes from scratch. But that's not quite true. In 2018 only one of the top twenty truly qualifies as a self-made businessman. Jim Ratcliffe (£21.05 billion), chair of the Ineos chemicals group, was raised in a Lancashire council house and was lucky to win a place at a grammar school. The rest of the top twenty all owe their wealth to a more fortunate set of life chances, suggesting that when it comes to getting rich we live in an inheritocracy rather than a meritocracy. Sri and Gopi Hinduja (£20.64 billion) inherited a trading empire from their late father. The father of Lakshmi Mittal (£14.66 billion) built a steel firm in India. Charlene de Carvalho-Heineken (£11.1 billion) inherited the brewing company founded by her great-grandfather in 1864. Hans Rausing (£9.33 billion) inherited half of Tetra Pak from his father. Kirsten and Jörn Rausing (£10.85 billion) inherited the other half from their father, Hans's brother. Guy and George Weston (£10.05 billion) were gifted a retailing company founded by their Canadian great-grandfather. The Duke of Westminster (£9.96 billion) and Earl Cadogan (£6.7 billion) inherited property empires. Ernesto Bertarelli (£9.66 billion) was handed the family's pharmaceutical business. (If you look very closely, you might see a pattern here!)

Rich entrepreneurs are exceptional individuals who have usually benefited from the advantages of education, family wealth and a privileged network. The *Sunday Times* rich list is meant to be aspirational, but the prospect of breaking into this class of billionaires is really only a mirage. For every successful self-made businessman or woman like Ratcliffe there are thousands more who don't make it. And for those individuals who do make a success out of their businesses, there is a strong tendency to justify it in terms of their personal input rather than other more random conditions. It has even got a name: survivorship bias.

American researchers conducted a unique study to show how this happens. Using a series of rigged games of

Monopoly, psychologist Paul Piff gave one randomly chosen player advantages over the rest – twice the money, rolling two dice instead of one each turn, and more cash for passing 'Go'.[9] After the game the winning player was asked to justify his success. Instead of acknowledging all the advantages they had been given, the winning players talked in terms of their clever property selection and hotel-buying strategy. Of course, making it as a business person is not quite the same as winning a rigged game of Monopoly. Yet there is good scientific research to show how business success or wealth creation has an almost totally random distribution throughout society. In a 2018 paper, 'Talent vs Luck: The Role of Randomness in Success and Failure', researchers concluded that: 'If it is true that some degree of talent is necessary to be successful in life, almost never the most talented people reach the highest peaks of success, being overtaken by mediocre but sensibly luckier individuals'.[10]

If you happen to have inherited a family business or a wealthy legacy, then the luckier you will be.

Equality of opportunity is a deceit perpetrated on a willing society blinded to the lottery of capitalism. Each person can only work a finite number of hours, and hard work only makes you rich if you can benefit from someone else's hours. To make money you need to exploit other people's time. So you have a much better chance of making a success out of your business if you can persuade someone else to perform the work *for* you.

The privileged business class has been able to circumvent the need to work at all by making use of equity and money markets, giving existing wealth a gravitational force that draws in even more money. If you can't pay other people to work for you and you haven't got any cash to invest, the odds are you won't get rich.

Today families with a self-employed member are twice as likely to become insolvent than one where family members have salaried employment.[11] The future doesn't look rosy for the next generation of entrepreneurs, either: between 2016 and 2019 the number of young people going bankrupt increased tenfold, and under 25 years of age now comprise 6.5 percent of all personal insolvencies.[12]

It doesn't have to be like this. The government needn't stand back and watch our high streets degenerate. The state needs to start supporting enterprise and investing in the next generation of shopkeepers, restaurateurs and hoteliers. People starting out in business need to have free access to financial advice and business planning. The success of a business should not be judged solely on the short-term profit it is generating. After all, businesspeople are taking incredible risks whether they are aware of it or not. They are also taking risks on behalf of *other* people. Other factors need to be taken into account when supporting start-ups. More consideration should be given to the number of people a business employs, how much it pays its staff and the quality of the working conditions and benefits. We need to reduce the random nature of capitalism and spread more of its success among more people. Successive governments have recognised the price of small businesses without ever understanding their value to the community, our society and the economy in the long term.

15

THE CITY

THE CLASSIC-CAR ENTHUSIAST
WHO FORGOT WHAT KIND OF CAR
HIS BROKER WAS DRIVING

Damien Booth has always loved cars. As a boy he collected Dinky models and in adult life he bought a 1957 Austin Healey sports car which he likes to drive along the leafy lanes of the Cheshire countryside on balmy summer weekends.

Damien is a qualified geologist who had to retrain as a business consultant after the collapse of the North Sea oil and gas market in the early 1990s. Since then he has been working at a Manchester-based energy company as a markets analyst. When he was made redundant by a well-known British oil company he also lost a slice of his future pension.

In 2015 Damien, a member of a Cheshire classic car driving club, met another enthusiast who took a shine to his Healey and offered him £100,000 to buy it. Although Damien loved his car dearly he always knew it was his rainy-day 'pension' and one day he would have to part with it. A hundred grand was a good offer, so Damien sold the car and prepared to invest the money in a basket of safe shares which he hoped would out-perform the pension annuity market and give him a healthy return on his investment. Damien had read about the pitfalls of trading in shares, especially for the novice investor. So, not taking any chances, he decided to consult a local stockbroker in Chester to advise him on his portfolio.

He chose a reassuringly old-fashioned firm and after an initial telephone call Damien was invited to a meeting with one of the managers. Half an hour early for the appointment, he was ushered into a grand drawing room at the front of an Edwardian former coaching house. As he sat on the unsprung, grey cotton sofa he passed the time watching the cars arriving and leaving the generously proportioned office car park. It soon occurred to Damien that while the brokers and their staff were driving top-of-the-range models, and in the senior partner's case a rather splendid 1950s Wolseley, the clients were not.

It would take several years, and several thousand pounds of his Healey money, before Damien would be able to make any sense of this observation.

Damien was advised by his brokers to invest in a safe basket of FTSE companies. For providing this service he was charged 1.5 percent. But the brokers also recommended a mutual fund, which pooled the shared investments of other clients, and he was charged a further 1 percent management fee. So Damien was now paying 2.5 percent of his £100,000 in fees. After 3 years his investments returned profits in dividends worth £19,000 but the brokers and mutual had creamed off £7,500 in fees. Damien also had to pay 32.5 percent in tax on his dividends.[1] And after deducting a further 1.5 percent for inflation over the 3 years he could see that he was barely breaking even. Damien was entitled to ask what exactly his brokers had done to earn themselves such a high return on his money, other than periodically writing a letter detailing the trading on his account and the general movements of the market. He discovered the answer: not much.

Nevertheless, since he accepted from the start of his engagement of the brokers that he needed specialist advice, he reasoned that there must be added value in protecting him from the dangers of the rise and fall of the markets. But he was wrong, because his financial advisers made sure they were paid an annual fee based on Damien's assets – *not* on the increased value of his investment. They were guaranteed to make a profit even when Damien was making a loss. All the risk was being borne by Damien.

Had he read a copy of Fred Schwed's wryly observed *Where Are the Customers' Yachts?*, published in 1940, the penny might have dropped sooner, saving him a considerable amount of anguish as well as some of his investment. Schwed's account of the relationship between the investment markets and the average investor revealed what everyone else suspected – that the only people getting rich in the City are the people *working* there.

'It took me 3 years to realise why the partners were the ones driving the expensive cars', said Damien.

★★★

It is estimated that global financial advisers are overcharging their clients by $250 billion a year for services that fail to even meet their own stated benchmarks. That's more than the US government will spend in a year on interest payments for a $16 trillion national debt.[2] And remember that the safer bonds and other fixed-income products typically yield less than 3 percent these days, causing advisory fees to eat up an even larger portion of returns.

Damien eventually wrote a letter to his brokers cancelling his dealings with the firm and requested the return of the control of his assets. The managing partner wrote back expressing disappointment at losing such a 'valued customer' but must have wondered deep down why more clients didn't do the same.

When Damien took custody of his shares it became apparent that his managers had barely touched them since the day he had first invested. Sickened by his experience of professional advisers, he decided to go it alone. After some rudimentary research he felt confident enough to make his own trades. He was glued to his computer watching his shares tick up and down in real time. In a daily sequence of reactive trades he sold and bought as he tried to second-guess the market. He soon found that the burden of active management of his portfolio was taking up too much of his time and causing him a great deal of anxiety:

> It got to the point where every free moment of my working and recreational day I was watching the FTSE. If I went out to lunch with a colleague or a client I would sneak into the toilets to make trades on my phone. At home I couldn't leave my phone alone. When the shares took a tumble I felt sick and when they shot up I was elated, quickly calculating how much I was profiting from my trades. To be absolutely honest it was ruining my life.

Damien was being driven by a common investor psychology which inverts the stock market maxim for sensible trading: 'buy low and sell high'. The emotional interference means most people, including many seasoned traders, tend to buy when the market is performing well and sell out of fear when the market starts to drop. 'I was a mess, and getting poorer'.

The truth is that even if Damien had found a way to silence his instincts, he was always operating against the odds.

Since 1926 half of all the world's shareholder profits has been derived from just 90 traded companies – 25,000 stocks failed to make any overall profit. And since 2005, 88 percent of global equity funds have failed to meet their benchmarks. But with the advent of the Big Bang[3] and high-frequency trading Damien imagined that he was now able to compete on level terms with the traders. After all, the trading app that he had downloaded to his phone mirrored what the brokers and fund managers now used to make *their* electronic bids.

It is true that since frenzied trading floors moved to computer data centres, the majority of deals in equities and futures are now executed by computers. But if anything this has widened the gap in the trading advantage between the City professional and the ordinary investor. The rise of high-frequency trading means that ordinary investors buying or selling stocks, bonds, exchange-traded funds or futures are betting against an algorithm that can make decisions and execute trades quicker than humans can blink. The fund managers and traders have invested in superfast wireless capacity, efficient computer switches and coding talent, allowing them to prey on the slower investors. In recent years the City has migrated from redundant fibre-optic cables to microwave towers that transmit data in 8 milliseconds.

Michael Lewis in his book *Flash Boys: A Wall Street Revolt* described how the inequality in trading arms has created 'a small class of insiders with the resources to create speed [who] were now allowed to preview the market and trade on what they had seen'.[4] His revelations led to calls for regulatory intervention to even up the trading playing field in finance centres all over the world. Yet the fair availability and access to price-sensitive information remains as elusive as it was in the analogue days of trading floors and secret hand signals.

Regulators must know they will never be able to cut the link between speed and profit. In December 2019 their impotence was laid bare by an embarrassing scandal at the heart of their own processes when it emerged that the Bank of England's press conferences were being secretly relayed to City firms 8 seconds before everyone else. The spoken words of the Governor of the Bank of England have the power to move markets. Anyone who had with an 8-second lead (light years in trading times) on what the Governor was saying could clean up. City firms were paying £5,000 a time for this service and making millions out of it.

Damien Booth decided to try to even up the odds and adapt his investment strategy by using his experience and knowledge as a geologist to research the markets he was interested in. He alighted on an Indian energy company that was waiting for the government's green light to develop a vast swathe of forested land containing gas and coal in the Punjab. When the announcement from the Indian energy ministry finally came through, Damien was duly alerted by one of the news feeds he had set up in his trading research tool.

He used half his investment (£50,000) to purchase shares in the energy company. But after a short climb the share began what would turn out to be a 6-month downward trajectory, wiping out half his £50,000. What Damien couldn't have known was that the energy company had no resources to exploit the Indian government's decision. In fact, it turned out the company was little more than a tax vehicle for an Indian family who had invested all their fortune in British commercial property. The directors never had any intention of mining the land. But as long as the company was set up as an energy investment company looking for lucrative new energy markets, it attracted investor interest:

> I couldn't understand why, despite all the information to the contrary and supported by rave reviews in the business press, this company was such a stinker. After 6 months I decided to get out and try to reconcile myself to the financial loss. I just couldn't afford to keep investing in it even though my head was telling me that any day now it would start making a profit.

Damien had fallen prey to another City maxim: an investor who can't stay solvent for as long as the market remains illogical will soon go bust.

So now Damien had been beaten twice – once by the financial advisory industry and once by the capricious power of the markets.

Yet the financial press is constantly telling us how investors have made fortunes through what appear to be superior analytical skills. Household names like Peter Lynch and Warren Buffett achieved their successes by picking individual stocks. But many individuals you've never heard of have attempted similar strategies and failed. Even most professional mutual fund managers can't beat the market.

Most that do are just exceptionally lucky. There are plenty of studies to show that a portfolio of randomly chosen stocks can perform as well as a carefully assembled one. The funds that do outperform the market are the ones that survive. Fund managers and asset managers rarely mention all the losing funds they have been forced to close. Many more suffer from something called 'closet indexation' where their funds have the appearance of being actively traded but are actually only mirroring the benchmarks.

Yes, you may be able to beat the market, but with investment fees, taxes and human emotion working against you, you're more likely to do so through luck rather than skill. If you can merely match the FTSE 500, with a transactional-fee deduction, you'll be doing better than most investors.

Studies show that if you really want to make any money in stocks and shares the best practice is to do nothing for long periods of time – which ironically was precisely the same policy employed by Damien's brokers.

And that was what Damien ended up doing – nothing: 'It changed everything. I got my life back, I started sleeping properly and I enjoyed just being in the moment. I may not have been generating particularly good returns but I wasn't taking big losses either'.

The City is set up like a casino and programmed by a super-computer so that the house always wins. It has done this by building in complexity to what should be a fairly straightforward business transaction – the buying and selling of physical things.

Once upon a time a farmer who wanted to sell her corn at the end of the harvest loaded it onto her wagon and went to market. Today that corn is sold long before it is harvested. It is sold as a right to buy the corn at a future date – which in turn is traded as an option to purchase the corn in the future. The contract to buy the corn can constitute an overly complex financial instrument called a swap. Swaps work like an insurance policy by allowing purchasers to buy protection against an unlikely but devastating event. Each swap involves two agreements rather than just one and requires corporations agreeing to exchange something of value (a contract to buy corn) with the expectation of exchanging back at some future date. Simply speaking, swaps give corporations the opportunity to shift the performance of their assets quickly and cheaply without actually changing ownership of those assets. Today swaps are an extremely popular method of managing risk and generating revenues.

But swaps have become so complex and so far removed from the real products to which they relate that no one – certainly not the banks or the regulators – really understands how they affect the financial markets. By 2007 their market value stood at $62.2 trillion. When the sub-prime mortgage crisis blew up in America in 2008 they acted like petrol poured onto a financial inferno.

Despite everything that has happened since then, the City remains addicted to complexity. The reason for this is that every part of complexity in a transaction attracts a separate charge or fee. And the fund management industry, worth £8 trillion, is the most egregious expression of this money-for-nothing culture.[5]

The individual hedge fund manager who best represents this 'emperor's new clothes' industry is Neil Woodford.

Just like all the other fund managers his profits came from the fees he charged his clients. But Woodford, once described as the investor who made Middle England rich and 'the man who can't stop making money', was forced to close his investment business, worth £15 billion, in 2019 after trapping hundreds of thousands of savers in his flagship fund and sparking Europe's biggest investment scandal for a decade.

The difference between Woodford and the rest of the fund management industry was that his customers found out he was a snake oil salesman and demanded their money back.

After years of seemingly having the Midas touch for tipping growth funds it turned out that he was no better at making money than someone like Damien.

Chris Sier, a former policeman and now champion for transparency fund managers' fees, has claimed that even straightforward investment involves 16 steps, for which the customer is charged a usually hidden fee. The independent financial adviser, the fund manager, custody bank (which manages equities) and the broker all take their cut. Even government-backed, tax-free individual savings accounts can attract exorbitant adviser and management fees that render them little better than building society accounts.

Sier has trained his attention on helping ordinary investors negotiate the investment industry.

In 2017 the Financial Conduct Authority appointed Sier to spearhead a drive to establish new standards for institutional investment fees. He refused to take a penny in payment for his new role, and shortly after starting in the post told the *Financial Times*: 'I don't think it is fair that anyone that works bloody hard – civil servants, teachers, nurses or a street sweeper – should end up with a pension that is less than it should be because of the inappropriate acquisition of their wealth through the very complex value chain that is the asset management industry'.

Sier, a professor at Newcastle University Business School who has spent more than a decade as a consultant advising pension funds and asset management companies, says: 'I know how an asset manager works. Every asset management company is a complex mixture of manual and automated processes. That complexity is a major contributor to costs and risks'.

He poignantly observes: 'Honesty can become a selection criterion for managers'.[6]

What happened to Damien is happening to everyone. The City's fees are taken from the pockets of savers. Every penny the City makes is paid for by people working outside the financial sector.

In its original incarnation the finance services industry was easy to read. Bankers charged for lending money and brokers charged for arranging the sale of contracts. Today it has grown into a behemoth of labyrinthine criss-crossing markets each relying on the other for their margins.

The volume of trade in foreign exchange alone is 100 times the volume of world trade in goods and services. The scale of exposures on financial 'derivative' contracts like swaps – those esoteric bets that financial institutions make between themselves – is today around three times the value of all the assets in the world.

Because the City doesn't actually produce anything apart from profit, it has to be constantly inventing new processes for creating wealth. And because there are so many City mouths to feed it spends that wealth as quickly as it creates it. Three-quarters of a million people work in London's finance sector. Half of them are employed in financial services jobs and the other half are in related professional services occupations. About 148,000 workers are employed in banking, 76,000 in insurance, 31,000 in fund management and 108,000 in other financial attendant roles. Within the professional services, 107,000 people are in accountancy, 181,000 are in management consulting and 100,000 are in legal services.[7]

The fees needed to pay for the City are estimated to be £268 billion a year, mostly paid in wages and bonuses for traders and fund managers.[8]

Over the decades the financial services market has become consumed by short-term investment and superfluous multiple transactions which generate extra fees and costs. Traders, bankers and fund managers have become hooked on short-term profits. This puts the market at odds with the long-term prosperity of the businesses which provide the tangible products the City bets on.[9]

It also eats into institutional investment funds, like pension funds, run for our benefit. By taking profits in fees at so many points in the management of funds, it restricts the growth of pension funds and raises concerns that millions of Britons will run out of money in their old age.

The only way the fund management market can really add value is by improving the performance of companies and institutional funds by offering them long-term investments. But that is not in their profitable interest. That is not what the City is for.

The financial services industry exists to organise the allocation of capital – taking savings and funnelling them to profitable investments. But the capital needs of business have changed over the past century. The physical manufacturing businesses made up of specialised plant and buildings have given way to the 'knowledge economy'. For example, neither of the tech giants Google or Facebook require the same financial services sold to hard-copy media companies. The business model for Amazon, the world's most valuable company, would be unrecognisable to the entrepreneurs of the past.

John Kay is an economist and author of *Other People's Money*. He says Facebook, Amazon, Apple, Google and Microsoft employ very little capital:

> They do not need to own the shops, offices and computers they use in their business, and mostly they don't. Even capital-intensive large businesses, such as Exxon and Shell, are self-financing. The stock market is no longer a means of putting money into companies but a means of getting it out.[10]

The financial services sector is fast becoming an unnecessary tax on the *non*-financial sector. The trend towards the consolidation of markets means today there are half the number of public companies there were 20 years ago, so there are fewer businesses for ordinary institutional and individual investors to invest in.

Kay says it is time to challenge the City about what it really does:

> There are good reasons to be sceptical about how much the financial sector contributes to Britain. It is an area in which Britain has competitive strengths, including language and time zone. Private profit without public benefit is a policy problem everywhere in finance, but a particularly acute British dilemma.[11]

The City needs to start investing in our future prosperity. After all, there is more profit to be made from long-term investments than short-term ones. Investors like Warren Buffett have proved that to be the case.

Kay argues that this is the moment for government to invest in the UK's underfunded roads, railways and public buildings:

> We could borrow for 50 years to renew our crumbling infrastructure at lower interest rates than at any time in history; instead it is attempting to keep bond and share prices high through buying existing debt back via quantitative easing.

Kay's vision includes a fundamental realignment of the pillars of the City:

> With large companies no longer needing external finance, the primary role of the stock market investor is stewardship – ensuring that Britain's businesses have effective management, well-thought-out strategy and a perspective that matches the time horizons of the savers whose life cycle and retirement plans depend on them.

He says we have locked ourselves into a 'dysfunctional cycle' of quarterly earnings reports, while 'too many executives enrich themselves at their investors' expense'. Fund managers compete to outperform each other in a market that delivers short-term wins at the expense of long-term economic stability:

> We need a simpler world in which unwieldy financial conglomerates are broken up into focused institutions, and in which short chains of intermediaries provide more direct links between savers and the assets in which their funds are

deployed. We need to restore 'boring' banks that take our deposits and short-term savings and lend them on to government and home buyers. And we need asset managers whom we can trust to hold our savings for the long term and build knowledgeable, enduring relationships with the companies in which they invest.[12]

Over 70 years ago Professor John Kenneth Galbraith, author of *The Affluent Society*, was saying exactly the same thing:

The study of money, above all other fields in economics, is one in which complexity is used to disguise truth or to evade truth, not to reveal it. The process by which banks create money is so simple the mind is repelled. With something so important, a deeper mystery seems only decent.[13]

16

WEALTH

THE WORLD-FAMOUS MOUNTAINEER WHO SLEEPS IN HIS FORD MONDEO

Ranulph Fiennes is this country's greatest explorer. He is a household name who has achieved worldwide fame by completing expeditions to the most inhospitable parts of the planet. His books are bestsellers and his speaking tours are sold out. Yet Fiennes is by no means a wealthy man.

Often the man who trekked to both poles and was the oldest human to climb the world's highest mountain finds it hard to pay his bills – so much so that he told the *Sunday Times* in 2019 he can only afford to own a beaten up Ford Mondeo, which he uses to drive himself to speaking events. And rather than spend a hundred pounds on a hotel room, he often elects to kip the night in the Mondeo. After the event Fiennes takes his box of books from the Mondeo's boot and hopes members of the audience, inspired by his talk, will show their appreciation by making a purchase:

As the family breadwinner I need to write a book every other year. But with tax and literary agent fees and the often considerable cost of research, it's not enough. My only regular non-literary income comes from giving lectures with colour slides. By taking on enough lecture commissions, I can just about cope financially between expeditions.

But of course Fiennes, who owns a farmhouse in Exmoor and benefits from a sponsorship deal with Land Rover, is by no means poor. He has yet to follow in the footsteps of World Cup football legends Bobby Moore, Nobby Stiles, Alan Ball and Gordon Banks, who became so hard up that they were forced to sell off their prized possessions – 1966 World Cup winners' medals. In fact, only four of the entire squad, including manager Sir Alf Ramsey, have made enough money since clinching the World Cup trophy to keep hold of their medals. Banks, in a foreshadowing of the housing crisis, used the £120,000 he received from his medals' sale to help his three children put down deposits to buy their first homes.

The failure of professional sportsmen and women to cash in on their celebrity and success is by no means a phenomenon consigned to the stars of the past. Carlton Cole played 16 years in the top flight of English football, at his peak earning £30,000 a week turning out for West Ham United. He also won seven caps for England. But in 2018 he was declared bankrupt after a series of poor financial investments. He is one of a growing number of well-paid footballers of the modern era who have hit financial rock-bottom, a list that includes England goalkeeper David James and England and Arsenal midfielder Paul Merson. Research by football magazine *FourFourTwo* has found that four out of ten footballers in the UK have careers that end in financial troubles.[1] It is even worse in America, where eight out of ten NFL players file for bankruptcy within 5 years of retiring from the game.[2] And we have already heard how the once multimillionaire tennis player Boris Becker ended up juggling debts.

Premier League footballers might be the first to spring to mind when you think of who is *really* rich, but there are plenty of examples of celebrities outside the world of sport who appear to be fabulously wealthy but are in fact stone broke. Perhaps the most famous is the former model and It girl Katie Price. In November 2019 a court declared her bankrupt after she failed to repay her debts. From the most successful explorer in the world to the greatest football team ever assembled, to pop stars and celebrities – all that glitters may not be gold.

Being rich is not the same as being wealthy. While wealth is a state of permanent riches, being rich is transient. The truly wealthy don't need to do anything to generate an income – their assets (properties and investments) do that job for them. The rich, however, are dependent on a salary or a business to make their money, and some careers have a perilously short window of opportunity. Being rich is only ever one misstep away from poverty.

Nevertheless, the illusion of a permanent state of wealth is being peddled like it has never been peddled before. Many of the people at the top – the kind you see at glitzy televised events – are often struggling to keep up *appearances* of glamour. The rest of us are trying to copy what we think their lives are like. If we can't have fame then we all want a chance to get the money. And if hard work won't make it happen then maybe the magic money tree will deliver.

A multi-billion-pound industry has been built on the back of 'get rich quick' schemes which promise ordinary investors to never have to work again but usually end with nobody getting rich apart from the architects and advisers to the scheme. Whether it's fake investment funds, dodgy currencies or advance-fee frauds the temptation to take a shortcut to riches has been around forever.

Bernie Madoff, the American financier who set up the largest Ponzi scheme in history, had been defrauding thousands of investors out of tens of billions of dollars for nearly 20 years. His con was actually quite simple: Madoff used new investors to pay off old investors which created an investment scheme out of a perpetual fraud. If it hadn't been for the 2008 financial crash, which exposed the lie upon which Madoff had built his fraudulent fund, it would probably still be going today. Instead Madoff was sent to prison for 150 years.

Those who had fallen for Madoff's con had done so for the same reasons as the investors who had been cheated by Charles Ponzi, the man who gave his name to the first Ponzi fraud in the 1920s. At a time when the annual interest rate for bank accounts was 5 percent, Charles Ponzi promised investors that he could provide a 50 percent return in just 90 days by investing in his postage stamp fund. Ponzi initially bought a small number of stamps to lend legitimacy to the scheme but then switched to using incoming funds from new investors to pay purported returns to earlier investors.[3]

One hundred years earlier Gregor MacGregor, a Scottish soldier and adventurer, conned British and French investors into investing in a fictional Central American state he named 'Poyais'. Hundreds invested their savings in 'Poyaisian' government bonds and land certificates, while about 250 emigrated to MacGregor's invented country in 1822–23, where they died from malaria in the jungles of the Mosquito Coast. MacGregor's Poyais scheme has been described as the most brazen confidence trick in history.

From MacGregor to Ponzi to Madoff, the story is always the same: people believe they can get rich by outsmarting the laws of the markets. Dr Joe Gladstone from UCL's School of Management puts it like this:

> People on average are overly optimistic. The average person thinks they are special, that bad things won't happen to them. People think they are unique. There is a difference between sophisticated and unsophisticated investors. There's going to be a lag between those people who do invest in technology companies who do make a lot of money and they can use strategy to make even more money by having unsophisticated people follow them and then bump up the stock in price and then sell.[4]

The growth of internet and social media investment opportunities has spawned a new class of dodgy stock.

The Bitcoin investment bubble which burst a long time ago is a very good example of how wealth is being promised to those foolish enough to believe there is still hope.

Jim Davidson is an old-style stand-up comedian from the 1980s. He hosted *Big Break* and *The Generation Game* before being declared bankrupt in 2006 unable to pay a £700,000 tax bill, and he's been pretty skint ever since, claiming to have spent £60 million over the years on ex-wives, bad investments and his children's expensive school fees.

But in 2019 an email and social media advertisement featuring Davidson went viral. It claimed that the comedian had bounced back from his financial disasters by investing in Bitcoin. The email ad was accompanied with a picture of Davidson on the TV show *Good Morning Britain* where it was claimed he told the hosts all about his successful Bitcoin investment. The ad read: 'Jim Davidson Reveals How He Bounced Back After the Bankruptcy – He claims anyone can do it & shows "Good Morning Britain" How!'

If an old-school stand-up comedian from the 1980s could cash in on the Bitcoin boom, then so could you, was the not-so-subtle implication. But of course it wasn't true. Davidson had not been on *Good Morning Britain* to talk about his new-found fortune and, just like many investors, he hadn't a clue what a Bitcoin was. Some people did make their fortune in Bitcoin but they had got in at the start, cashed in their winnings and were already investing in much safer and much more traditional stocks. Those who followed on, hopeful of reaping rewards from the Bitcoin bubble, lost their shirts.

Fraudsters are increasingly using social media sites to entice victims into making fake investments. And one of the more popular ruses is to fake celebrity endorsements. Thousands of these online scam adverts on Facebook have featured the personal finance expert Martin Lewis, whose name appeared next to a myriad of scam adverts for 'getting rich quick'. But Lewis decided to make a heroic one-man stand to try to force Facebook to do more to stop fraudsters using its site to rip off the public. In April 2018 the MoneySavingExpert. com founder issued High Court proceedings for defamation against Facebook after the company had failed to take action against the fraudsters abusing his name or image on the site. Lewis only ended his legal action when the social media firm agreed to settle his case out of court with a £3 million payout to set up a new anti-scams initiative run by Citizens Advice and create a smart scam ads reporting tool on Facebook.

The number of investment frauds reported in the first 6 months of 2019 hit 8,153 – almost double the amount from the same period the year before, according to the City of London Police's National Fraud Intelligence Bureau. Some of these frauds, such as Ponzi and pyramid schemes, are very familiar. But lawyers warn it is the growth in the new, unregulated 'shadow savings market' in the UK which is helping drive an increase in financial investments fraud.

One of the chief reasons is the emergence of the new cryptocurrencies, like Bitcoin. International law firm Pinsent Masons says it was the rising price of cryptocurrencies in 2017 which led to a surge in investing in worthless stocks. While some people got very rich, many more lost everything. Pinsent's partner Alan Sheeley is in no doubt that social media, as well as online stock price comparison sites which attract new and inexperienced investors, are driving up fraud in this area:

Fraudsters are taking advantage of investors' need for income. Suppressed interest rates on mainstream savings products have driven retail investors towards higher-yielding, more lightly regulated investments. Combined with the ease for companies of reaching the mass market through online advertising, this has added a new layer of risk for retail investors.

A feature of the unregulated 'shadow savings market' is aggressive advertising and marketing of investment products to inexperienced investors. This is being done in a variety of ways, including through price comparison sites and social media channels.[5]

Regulators are trying to clamp down on these kinds of fraudulent investments. In 2019 the Financial Conduct Authority had to intervene 225 times to tell firms to withdraw or change misleading advertising.

But fraud is only part of the trap for people who want to take the shortest route possible to getting rich. Each year hundreds of books are published by authors who claim to be able to pass on the secret formula for getting rich just for the cost of the cover price. Yet what they convey is little more than aphorism and anecdote laced with common sense freely available to anyone who has ever had a job. Very few authors mention the sheer *luck* of getting rich or that the best thing you can do is to have the good fortune of being born wealthy. Other authors share their insights on the secrets of investing and business success.

One of them is Warren Buffett's daughter-in-law. A former professional singer, Mary Buffett married Warren Buffett's son Peter in 1980 and divorced him 13 years later. She has since published a number of business advice books invoking the Buffett name, including her latest *7 Secrets to Investing Like Warren Buffett*. She has co-written eight other books about her father-in-law's investment strategies. They are:

- *The Tao of Warren Buffett: A Collection of Pithy and Inspiring Sayings from America's Favorite Businessman That Reveal His Secrets of Success*
- *The Warren Buffett Stock Portfolio. Warren Buffett Stock Picks: Why and When He Is Investing in Them*
- *Buffettology*
- *The New Buffettology: The Proven Techniques for Investing Successfully in Changing Markets That Have Made Warren Buffett the World's Most Famous Investor*
- *Warren Buffett and the Interpretation of Financial Statements: The Search for the Company with a Durable Competitive Advantage*

- *Warren Buffett's Management Secrets: Proven Tools for Personal and Business Success*
- *Warren Buffett and the Art of Stock Arbitrage: Proven Strategies for Arbitrage and Other Special Investment Situations*
- *The Buffettology Workbook: Value Investing the Warren Buffett Way*

None of these books *guarantee* business success, of course, but you can see how by associating herself with the world's most famous investor Mary Buffett has become a bestselling author. She was already an experienced businesswoman before she married into the Buffett family. After her divorce she became a consultant to Fortune 500 companies, helped launch the Sanford DeLand UK Buffettology fund and founded the Buffett Online School. She has also taught business and finance at UCLA and other California state universities. But if Mary Buffett is really so good at finance, why doesn't she write about it using her maiden name?

Lessons about how Warren Buffett made and kept his fortune are best coming from the horse's mouth. Buffett lives in the same house that he bought with his wife when he started out in the 1940s. He doesn't own much property because he says it is just something else to worry about. He likes to point out:

The only difference between me and you is the quality of long distance travel that I buy [he uses his wealth to purchase first class air and train travel]. I won the lottery when I was born in America – fifty to one chance of being born in the US. I could have been born in India or Africa, and how much harder it would be to harness my potential.

His advice to the successful investor of today is: 'divorce yourself from the fears and greed of the people around you'.

We have seen how real wealth and the appearance of wealth are two very different things. And we have seen how being a pop star, sporting legend or even this country's greatest living explorer does not guarantee riches. Celebrities and national heroes may be able to sustain the illusion of wealth in the good times, supported by endorsements and branding freebies, but ultimately their grasp on a comfortable, high-financed life-style is fleeting.

Public displays of wealth have cast a spell on us all. The more they desperately cling to their celebrity trappings, the more we all believe what they have must be *worth* having. We know we may never circumnavigate the world or write a hit single, but we can still make our fortunes as super-influencers, YouTube sensations or Bitcoin millionaires. Even if we choose a more orthodox business model there are plenty of get-rich-quick schemes promising to shorten the odds and speed up the wealth-creation process. But of course there are no guaranteed shortcuts – just a valueless industry making money out of selling us the *illusion* of wealth. And because now all this false hope is marketed behind the veneer of the internet, we can't see the tricksters, con artists and shysters in their bedrooms, sitting in their underpants, spewing out spam and preying on our greed.

17

WINNERS

THE NUMISMATIST WHO
ACCIDENTALLY CORNERED THE MARKET

Henry Saltwood knows how to enjoy life. Every year, on the anniversary of his marriage, he invites and pays for all his old university mates to stay at one of Europe's most famous hotels, Harry's in Venice. While his friends enjoy the hospitality of a plush Venetian hotel, Henry and his wife spend the week enjoying the opulence of the nearby Gritti Palace, where a night's stay costs £500, twice the price of a room at Harry's. The message is not very subtle, but few of Henry's uni mates are in a position to turn down a free holiday to Venice including paid flights and bar bills.

What Henry lacked in social status while at university and on through the years he was grafting away to train as a chartered accountant, he has more than made up for with the largesse he now showers on his friends.

The story of Henry's rise to wealth began when he was working for a firm of accountants just after Tony Blair decided to make the Private Finance Initiative (PFI) a key part of his public infrastructure investment policy. This was New Labour's solution to chronic underinvestment in public services, which had been so obvious during the neglect of previous administrations.[1] PFIs permit private companies to contract with the government on major public building projects. Although PFIs were packaged as risky ventures, there was actually very little risk in play. The many safety clauses written into the contracts ensured that PFI companies were effectively indemnified against loss. Henry saw the PFI for what it was – free money. So he left his accountancy practice and set up a project management and investment company which won a series of PFI contracts to build hospitals and schools in the South of England. By 2007 he was a very wealthy man and had retired before his fortieth birthday with an extremely generous pension and a multi-million-pound investment portfolio.

Henry hired expensive accountants to help him manage his wealth. Before long he had split his investments between the tax havens of the Caribbean and the high-interest accounts run by Britain's best-known fund managers. Henry, a law-abiding man who prided himself on never having incurred so much as a parking ticket, queried the legality of tax havens with his accountants but was told quite categorically that his investment choices contravened no UK or international regulations. Ethically it was a matter of personal preference. Given that all his friends, advised by a select group of professional advisers, were using the same complex investment vehicles and exotic financial jurisdictions, it didn't cross his mind that he had other choices. Treating himself as a business, Henry had a responsibility, almost a fiduciary duty, to maximise his responsibly earned wealth. And he had long ago stopped being surprised about how little tax he was paying for what turned out to be very profitable investments. Moreover, under the terms of the PFI contracts, his old company continued to be paid 1 million pounds a year even after the work had been completed.

Instead of retiring to live quietly with his wife and children by the sea, more and more of his time was taken up finding inventive ways to invest his burgeoning wealth. Because he was conscientious, he ensured that his money made *more* money by investing in more lucrative ventures and investment funds. Before long he had so much money that he was running out of things to do with it. So he took up numismatics and started collecting rare coinage bearing the head of Edward VIII who abdicated in 1937. He invested in a state-of-the-art strongroom, dug into the cellar of his Kensington home, as well as a very expensive security system. Then in 2019 Henry decided to sell his coin collection so that he could buy paintings and dabble in the fine-art market. And this was when he ran into a problem. Because Henry had acquired so many Edward VIII coins his financial advisers told him he had in effect cornered the market. If he were to sell his personal collection, he risked crashing the market and attracting unwanted publicity.

★★★

Henry wasn't greedy, just the happy beneficiary of a capital investment scheme that made rich people even richer. PFI contracts for NHS hospital projects alone will continue to pay out £55 billion to people like Henry until 2050. The initial £13 billion investment by a PFI company in new hospitals will end up costing the NHS in England a staggering £80 billion by the time all contracts come to an end.[2]

Henry's story illustrates how easy it is for a group of trained specialists to get very rich very quickly. To those uninitiated in complex finance, PFI may have looked like a fair bargain. But to Henry it was obvious that what the government was offering with PFI was a golden contract that in fact was almost risk-free.

As we have already discovered, the City is awash with people like Henry – bankers, lawyers and accountants – all earning multi-million-pound fees in a market that has no basis in reality. Today's twenty-first-century deal-making boom makes it the most rewarding time in history to be a professional adviser. It is impossible to make money without the help of this small group of specialist wealth shamans – the financial adviser, the accountant, the lawyer and, in the digital age, the adviser who understands 'big data'. Their astronomical fees are plucked from thin air to support the illusion that the trade in acquisitions can only be completed with the incantations and rituals practised by an initiated band of City insiders.

Their unique skill is understanding the rules of wealth creation and, for a share of this wealth, applying it to an individual's business or investment. If a business wants to trade for the chance to grow, then they have to pay off the advisers. Without their services businesses and the man-on-the-street investor can't enter the market and will find it even harder to get rich.

And who are they servicing? Who is paying the wages of the extraordinarily rich bankers, lawyers, accountants and PFI consultants?

Step forward the global super-rich, a motley collection of industrialists, hedge fund managers, institutional investors, energy magnates, social media moguls, old-fashioned family money, oligarchs and even a smattering of Bitcoin tycoons. As part of the globe's richest 1 percent they now own half the world's wealth. Or to measure it another way, the twenty-six richest billionaires control as many assets as the 3.8 billion people who make up the poorest half of the planet's population.[3]

These men (and occasional women) dictate so much of our economic future but are rarely seen in public. That is apart from one notable occasion: in the third week of every new year these plutocrats gather in the Swiss Alps at a ski resort called Davos. Entrance is by invitation only and mere millionaires need not apply. Access is strictly graded on a balance of global importance and wealth. The lowest entry level is a Davos badge restricting the bearer to hanging out in the Davos hotel foyer.[4] In this way Davos offers the super-rich a unique opportunity to flaunt their wealth in the faces of politicians while advising them on how to bend the rules further so they can make even more money – and all far from the prying eyes of the public.

When they gathered in 2020 they were able to report that their fortunes had doubled since 2010. A decade after the economy went into meltdown and millions of workers were losing their shirts, the richest of the rich have not only bounced back from financial catastrophe but have made even more eye-popping profits. David Rubenstein,[5] the American founder of the private equity group Carlyle, has doubled his wealth ($3.5 billion) since 2009, while Jamie Dimon,[6] who runs JPMorgan Chase, the largest bank in the US in terms of assets, was able to show he had more than tripled his net worth ($1.7 billion). And Stephen Schwarzman,[7] Donald Trump confidant and founder of private equity firm Blackstone, had increased his wealth sixfold ($18.2 billion).[8]

In fact in just 5 years membership in this exclusive club has become a little less exclusive. Since 2013 the global billionaire population has doubled from 1,140 billionaires to 2,311 billionaires in 2019.[9]

They may choose to meet in Switzerland but their favourite place to live is London. More billionaires are based in London than any city in the world. Despite the darkening economic outlook before the coronavirus, the global population of those ultra-high-net-worth individuals (UHNWIs) was forecast to rise by 22 percent over the next 5 years, meaning an extra 43,000 people will be worth more than $30 million by 2023.

Henry Saltwood justifies his fortune in terms of his unique abilities – intelligence, hard work and sound judgement. Who among us who had the good fortune to recognise what Henry understood about PFI in the 2000s would have acted any differently and not justified their success in the same terms? But as we have discovered, talent tends to be less important than luck when it comes to getting rich. Henry was lucky enough to have parents who could pay for him to attend a private school and shoulder the financial burden of university fees. Henry was also very fortunate to have qualified as an accountant and win a job in a top firm of accountants at a time when golden contracts in PFI were being handed out by Tony Blair's government. Henry's family had been making money for generations. Henry grew up immersed in the unwritten rules and culture of the financial services industry and the markets it serves. And he was not only schooled in how to make money; he was also taught how to keep hold of it.

The business pages of newspapers are littered with stories of people who have made a million and then lost it. Unless the same financial discipline is applied to the skills required for the accumulation of wealth as it is to its retention, a businessperson or entrepreneur can soon be separated from their fortune. How do we know this? The best evidence is what happens to lottery winners, ordinary people who are handed millions in random winnings.

Take Roger Griffiths and his wife Lara. Roger was an IT manager and Lara worked as a teacher until they won £1.8 million in 2005 in the national lottery. Eight years later the money had all gone and they were paying off debts. Predictably some of their fortune went on extravagances: lavish holidays to Dubai, Monaco and New York; weekend breaks in top London hotels; designer handbags, sports cars, expensive hairdos. As Lara told a television documentary in 2014: 'It couldn't have happened to a more enthusiastic spender. I went shopping'. But they also made sounder investments in property, a beauty salon business and their children's private education. And yet they still ended up broke.

Studies show that lottery winners are significantly more likely than non-winners to declare themselves bankrupt within 3–5 years after receiving their cheques. This is partly because they haven't learnt or acquired the financial discipline that keeps rich people rich.[10] What most lottery winners haven't been taught is that the rich don't live off income in the sense we understand (i.e. salaries, commissions and bonuses). The rich are the rentier class: they hold bonds, stocks and property, they lend, they rent – and income simply accrues.[11]

Education is the key starter to making and keeping wealth. At Britain's top private schools families ensure that pupils mix with other influential families who help each other make money. Going to the right school is an essential entrée to the business of making money in adult life. For instance, after David Cameron became prime minister in 2010, a posed picture emerged of his Eton peer group. His forty-five house-mates and housemaster are photographed in 1984 in white bow-tie uniform arranged in four tiers and squinting into the sun. It could have been taken in a different era, and it is notable that there is not a single black or brown face among them, but it is still interesting to know how each of those boys used his Eton education:

Ten of them went into the City, taking lucrative jobs with banks like Barclays Wealth, HSBC, Hambros and Merrill Lynch. Two had successful careers in industry with Land Rover and Cisco. At least three are entrepreneurs, one of whom founded Crussh, the chain of bars selling healthy food and drink. Five secured top jobs in journalism and publishing, with one becoming political editor of *The Times*. Two went into the arts; an owner of an Oscar-nominated British film company and an orchestra director. Three became leading lights in the fine-art market, with one securing a position as head of masters at Christie's. Two are successful architects. One is a chartered accountant and another is head of European research at upmarket estate agents Savills. One became a senior diplomat. Two are full-time aristocrats busy managing their country seats. One joined the army where he rose to the rank of lieutenant colonel.

The vast majority of the boys who gathered on that warm June afternoon to pose for their picture followed in the fine traditions of Eton and became leaders and front runners in their fields. But there are certain well-regarded professions that are, shall we say, very conspicuous by their absence. There are no scientists, inventors, doctors, probation officers, policemen or social workers. Etonians are not drawn to the public sector in the same way they are attracted to the wealth of the City, business or the professions.

Only one of the forty-six Eton boys chose a job serving the local community. In this respect the City hasn't really moved on since the days of the first London banking crisis of 1825 when a public school education was a non-negotiable prerequisite for a well-paid job in Threadneedle Street. Today private education plays just as big a part in the recruitment of bankers and private equity executives.

In 2014 a report for the Sutton Trust by the Boston Consulting Group found that over 50 percent of leaders of major banks and nearly 70 percent of heads of private equity firms were privately educated, while for new banking and private equity recruits the figures were 34 and 69 percent, respectively.[12] Privately educated bankers tend to hire privately educated bankers, a situation even more likely in private equity. A Social Mobility Commission report into access in investment banking reveals why these applicants are likely to be successful. It found that hiring managers have a tendency to 'recruit for familiarity and similarity', and focus on how they perceive someone will fit in.[13] The commission concluded that this mounts a particular challenge for candidates from disadvantaged backgrounds, as it suggests the concept of 'fit' is often determined by 'whether aspirant bankers share a social educational background with current hiring managers'. Entrance is now so skewed that pupils from ten named public schools are 100 times more likely to apply for the most prestigious business graduate schemes than their peers educated at the bottom 10 percent of schools, regardless of which universities they graduated from.

The middle classes, nobility and aristocracy have combined with the City to hold on to the nation's riches. Today Britain is ranked sixth (14,367) in the world in terms of number of UHNWIs, those with assets of more than $30 million (£26.5 million). America (240,575) and China (61,587) are the unsurprising runaway league leaders. But Germany, which at the end of the Second World War was on its knees, negotiated a costly reunification in the 1990s and more recently has absorbed millions of refugees, can lay claim to be domicile to the third (23,078) highest number of UHNWIs, closely followed by France (18,776).

Across the globe the story is of a self-perpetuating select group of already very rich people amassing extraordinary fortunes. In 2019 a record 31,000 individuals became members of the ultra-rich as they benefited from rising global stock markets and increased property prices. The total number of UHNWIs stands at 513,244, a rise of 6 percent from 2018.[14] That means there are more ultra-wealthy people around the world than the populations of Iceland, Malta or Belize. Those half a million people own 13 percent of the global wealth, almost $5 trillion of which is sitting in undisclosed, offshore bank accounts.[15] This all goes to show that the ultra-rich, by relying on armies of tax consultants, accountants and lawyers, have a tighter grip on their wealth than ever before. If we all want to get a little richer, then we will need to find ways of parting them from their excessive fortunes.

18

GENERATION POOR

THE GRADUATE WHO DIDN'T WANT TO MOVE TO LONDON

It has been 4 years since Ben Jackson finished his history and philosophy degree at the University of St Andrews. Ben had worked hard at school and then at sixth form college to win a coveted place at St Andrews, where he mixed with under-graduates from the top public schools including Eton College and Marlborough College, the school of choice for suitors to royal princes. Ben carried on in the same determined vein at university, studying for long hours, cutting back on his social life and finally graduating with a 2:1 degree and a clutch of very good academic references. Four years later he's jobless, with £62,000 of student debt and living back with his parents in Cockermouth, Cumbria. His prospects are uncertain as he decides what to do next with his life.

Ben's story is no different to hundreds of thousands of students who went to university hoping to leverage an investment in further education by turning £9,000 a year tuition fees into a reasonably paid job. Well that just hasn't happened for Ben:

> I tried qualitative market research because it seemed inter-esting, more of a challenge if you like, than just ringing people from a call centre. I gave journalism a go too, but after

writing to all the papers and TV companies round here I got nothing, even when I was only asking for work experience.

Market research opportunities have been more promising than journalism and even led to a couple of interviews. But he didn't make it on to any shortlists.

Although Ben widened his search for jobs outside the northwest, he didn't bother trying London or any of the big research companies based in the south:

I was born in the north and have lived here all my life. I feel part of this region and I don't want to move away down south. One company I wrote to in Lancaster said there might be something in their London office if I fancied applying. But I didn't bother. It might have been a foot on the ladder but the pay was so bad I didn't see how I would have been able to afford to live. I haven't got any savings and my parents are as broke as I am. All I'm looking for is an interesting, reasonably well-paid job close to my family.

To make ends meet Ben has been working in a nearby chocolate factory as a food packer, where he's paid the minimum wage, most of which he gives to his parents to pay his share of the bills:

If I could find something better I would have left a long time ago. The working conditions at the factory are shit. They make us wear coloured polythene berets so the managers know what level of experience we are. Red is for trainee, blue for intermediate and black for the most senior. If you're a black cap then you get an extra 15-minute break in the afternoon. The packing is pretty mindless; doesn't matter what colour hat you're wearing, we're all just ramming chocolate bars into boxes and loading them onto trolleys. You have to account for every minute you are on the premises – even toilet breaks. And the managers set workers against each other by promising promotion to those who work hard or volunteer for night shifts or extra shifts. When I first arrived I was told I could eat as much chocolate as I liked during my lunch and tea breaks. And I did. Now I'm sick to death of the taste of chocolate; can't eat it at all.

Ben's parents are worried about their son. In the past year they noticed him withdrawing into himself. He has been much less communicative and prone to mood swings. Margaret, his mum, says:

He doesn't even keep up with his university friends anymore. It's not good for him to still be living with us at his age. He's nearly thirty. He should have a place of his own, living with people of his own age. I think we bring him down. But he can't afford anything. The thing that seems to bother him most is the £62,000 he still owes. He gets a statement each year from the government and the debt just keeps getting bigger. Even if he got a decent job now he'd still have that money hanging over him. His dad has stopped talking to him about his career because it irritates him so much and he gets all aggressive about it. We are worried about him.

Six months after I spoke to Margaret I heard that Ben had made it on to a graduate shortlist for a market researcher's role for a well-known polling company in Manchester.

I could almost feel the relief in Margaret's voice. But when he turned up for the interview, Ben wasn't wearing his suit and he hadn't bothered shaving. Needless to say he didn't get the job. Margaret told me that she thought he had given up on any career or a way out of Cockermouth. The Jackson family believe their son is simply psychologically crushed by even the modest terms of his own ambition.

A university degree used to be a ticket to a good job and a good salary. It is how most people improved their financial circumstance. Graduates of all ages up to 64 years earn, on average, £10,000 more per year than non-graduates, according to the Department for Education's own research.[1] But since the global financial crisis this headline figure masks a much bleaker employment landscape for many young graduates. ONS figures from 2019 show that a third of graduates are overqualified for their job, with students of the arts, biology and humanities the most likely to be overeducated. That includes 22 percent of those who graduated before 1992 and 34 percent of those who graduated in 2007 or later.

The ONS report said that the incidence of overeducation for the 35–49 years age group was strong evidence that overeducation is now a persistent phenomenon in the UK labour market. And there is a price to be paid for being a graduate in the *wrong* job. The report's authors found: 'There is a wage penalty associated with overeducation; although overeducated employees earn positive return on wages, this is significantly lower compared with those who are matched to their jobs'.[2]

Hundreds of thousands of these underemployed graduates, like Ben Jackson and Alex King, whom we heard about in Chapter 7, not only have to cope with the failure of securing a job that matches their qualifications – they are also weighed down with huge debt. The total value of outstanding student loans at the end of March 2019 reached £121 billion and is predicted to rise to £450 billion (2018–19 prices) by the middle of this century.[3] These crippling debts are kept high, much higher than inflation, by extortionate interest rates. From 1 September 2019, for students from England and Wales who started university in or after 2012, the headline student loan interest rate was 5.4 percent, a figure greater than most mortgages and far higher than student loans from prior cohorts.

An undergraduate who started university in 2013 on full tuition fees and maintenance loans would in 2018 have owed £44,000. A student on the pre-2012 scheme would owe little more than half that (£25,000). Each year the loan remains unpaid, a further £4,500 in interest is added to the student's bill. Sneakily, the government uses the higher Retail Price Index for inflation to fix student loan interest while choosing to use the lower Consumer Price Index rate to dictate any state pension or benefits increases.[4] This matters because, for some graduates, the amount in added interest is more than their annual repayment – so the loan never gets paid off.

Under the scheme, the more you earn after graduation the more you pay back, which also means the loan repayments act as a tax on financial success. This, in turn, creates a built-in incentive to earn less. No wonder so many graduates, like Ben Jackson, have given up on finding a career.

Graduates aren't getting rich in America either: the student loan crisis is so bad that it is just about the only issue which unites Republicans and Democrats. More than 45 million Americans have student loans, and student debt has doubled over the past decade such that the overall national student debt has now reached $1.6 trillion, rising to $2 trillion by 2022. US student loan debt exceeds both credit card debts and car loans, and appears to be damaging the entire economy by causing young people to put off marriage, childbirth, home ownership and small business start-ups.

The knock-on effect of all this debt is felt hardest by the poorest students. UK government figures show that a pupil from a disadvantaged background is now less likely to go to university than their wealthier peers than at any point in the past decade. Just over a quarter (26.3 percent) of pupils eligible for free school meals went on to university in 2018, compared with 44.9 percent of those who were not on free school meals, according to data published by the Department for Education. That gap between the two groups – 18.6 percentage points – is the widest it has been since 2006–07. It's easy to see how this gap has grown: students from wealthy families don't tend to bother with student loans. After all, why would anyone bind themselves to these extortionate interest rates if they didn't have to.

The greatest difference between the young rich and the young poor is most pronounced in London. Remember how Ben Jackson had considered moving to the capital to find a job that matched his degree but then pulled back – partly because he was unwilling to leave his birth region and partly because of the economics of living in London? A report published in 2020 shows his instincts were right: using London School of Economics data, the Sutton Trust found that the idea of going to London to 'move up in the world' has become a 'myth'.[5]

Sir Peter Lampl, founder of the Sutton Trust, says London has become 'off limits' to ambitious people from poorer backgrounds who, like Ben, grew up outside the capital.

'Those that benefit most from opportunities in London', says Lampl, 'were either born there or are the economically privileged from other parts of the country'. The latter group can take advantage of career development ladders which are unavailable to young people without means. In London, where the highest-paid jobs are concentrated, the unpaid internship is still a popular route to getting a foot on the ladder of professional success. The media, publishing, finance, marketing, the law all recruit in this way. But how many debt-strapped graduates can afford to work for free in the world's most expensive city?

The unpaid internship is one reason a typical 25-year-old graduate from a poorer background earns £1,664 less than their contemporaries who have grown up in the capital's wealthiest homes, according to the Social Market Foundation. The gap widens to £7,904 between top-earning middle-class graduates and high-flying graduates from deprived backgrounds. Factors that create a 'class ceiling' include a lack of social connections or work experience, and hiring practices being subconsciously slanted against those from lower socio-economic backgrounds, warns the think tank.[6]

There is also plenty of evidence to show that doing well at university only takes you so far. Research by the IFS in 2014 compared privately educated and state-educated graduates who went to the same university and achieved the same degrees. It found that the privately educated graduate was earning £1,500 more than their state counterpart just 3 years after graduating.[7]

It may be disheartening to learn that family wealth is still a crucial factor in determining a young person's chance of getting rich. But in a society which allows money to talk that has always been the case. What has changed is the long-term economic prospects of our younger generations.

From a young person's perspective it is easy to believe that their future has been rigged in favour of older generations who already have everything. The baby-boomer generation, born after the Second World War and into the mid-1960s, stands accused of hogging the best jobs and all the houses. In his book, *The Pinch: How the Baby Boomers Took Their Children's Future – And Why They Should Give it Back*, the then Tory minister David Willetts declared: 'The charge is that the boomers have been guilty of a monumental failure to protect the interests of future generations'.[8] Ten years later he revisited his analysis with a new edition of his book and found that prospects for the younger generations were even more dire than he had first predicted.

In his updated book Willetts says young millennials are on course to pay more and receive less from the UK's education, health and benefit systems than any other post-war cohort, while baby-boomers are set to gain the most. Willetts, now president of the Resolution Foundation, concludes:

> When I first wrote *The Pinch* 10 years ago, I wanted to sound a warning siren that huge intergenerational injustices were opening up across Britain, and that young people were losing out while my generation was doing well. Ten years on, those divides have got worse. Young people have been short-changed by a lack of decent pay growth, a lack of decent,

affordable homes, and a state that expects them to pay more in order to receive less.

His findings showed that all cohorts born since 1931 are set to receive a 'welfare dividend' over the course of their lives by receiving more support from the welfare state, on average, than they have paid in taxes. But crucially the size of that dividend depends on when you were born. The biggest beneficiaries will be baby-boomers who he estimates are set for a 'welfare dividend' of £291,000 over the course of their lives – paying on average £941,000 worth of tax and receiving £1,231,000 worth of public services from the welfare state in return. By contrast, the smallest post-war beneficiaries are millennials born after 1996 like Ben Jackson. They will receive a far smaller 'welfare dividend' of just £132,000 (£962,000 of tax paid for £1,095,000 worth of public service benefits).

Because there are comparatively fewer millennials, tax revenues are insufficient to meet the growing expenses of public services enjoyed by the larger baby-boomer cohorts. Younger generations are already coping with lower benefit support compared with older generations while pensioner benefits continue to be protected by the generous triple lock on their state pension. Under an intergenerational law of diminishing returns, the economically active generations will, at some point in the next decade, heroically fail to pay the dues for both their own escalating consumption of health and welfare provision and those of their non-contributing parents and grandparents.

Willetts says that too often politicians have exacerbated age divides in the labour market and housing market by tilting the state ever further towards older generations. He wants to see the government embark on a policy programme to heal Britain's age divides and tackle our housing crisis, helping young people build up savings, and secure a sustainable funding system for social care that is fair to all generations.[9]

But it might be already too late to arrest the intergenerational inequality. Debts and low pay have hit millennials hard. Not only are millions being prevented from using education to help them get rich, they are also being sanctioned by the system. Most concerning is the number of young people under thirty who are being dragged into debt and then finding their careers blighted by the courts when they can't pay it back.

Court records show that in 2019 around 160,000 people in their twenties were given County Court judgments in England and Wales. That's a third more than the year before and the highest figure since records began. Young people are being chased by the courts for increasingly trivial amounts on mobile phone bills, missed energy payments or council tax demands. The civil servant in charge of compiling these figures is Mick McAteer, Chairman of Registry Trust. He is not given to bouts of hyperbole. So when he concludes that the latest figures 'show that a growing number of vulnerable households are facing severe financial strain', we must take him seriously.[10] Many young people who have debt judgments entered against them only find out they have been sanctioned when they are applying for jobs, loans or even mortgages – by then the damage has already been done. In this way young careers are being snuffed out before they have even got started.

There is no indication that our children's economic prospects are likely to improve. In fact, the latest research[11] shows that 600,000 more children are living in relative poverty than in 2012. At the age of sixteen, only 24.7 percent of disadvantaged students achieve a good pass in English and Maths GCSE compared with 49.9 percent of all other pupils. And half of all adults from the poorest backgrounds receive no training or further education at all after leaving school.

The 2020 pandemic has undoubtedly made a bad situation even worse as disadvantaged children missed out on vital classroom education, slipping further behind more privileged pupils.

Since the spring 2020 lockdown an additional 900,000 children have claimed free school meals, taking the total number of participants beyond 2.2 million – incredibly that is one in three of all schoolchildren aged 8 to 17.[12] A high-profile campaign spearheaded by Manchester United and England footballer Marcus Rashford warned the government that these growing numbers of starving children would critically damage the cognitive and physical development of a future generation. The government initially chose to look the other way. Today the chances of our children getting rich have never looked more bleak.

19

CORONAVIRUS

THE MAN WHO TRIED TO BUY
SOME TOILET PAPER

Remember Darren Reid, the 34-year-old man on benefits all his life who couldn't even afford to attend his own mother's funeral? I saw him again in March 2020, just as panic-buying swept across Britain. By the time Darren had cashed his cheque from the DWP, his two local supermarkets had completely sold out of toilet paper. Food was being rationed and all the BOGOF deals had been withdrawn:

> It's fucking ridiculous; the only toilet paper left is the fancy quilted stuff which is about three times the price of the economy rolls. I just want a Pot Noodle and some paper to wipe my arse on. Can you fix me up with a food bank voucher or something?

I had known Darren long enough to recognise that the barrage of expletives was symptomatic of high stress.

Darren Reid was one of millions of people in Britain already dependent on benefits who had got used to living a hand-to-mouth existence while waiting for state benefits and charity handouts. In a matter of a few days in March 2020 the poorest and most disadvantaged members of society suddenly found themselves even further back in the queue.

Since then nearly 2.5 million more Britons have applied and been granted UC, which just shows how precarious so many people's working lives had become. Hundreds of thousands of others have blown their meagre savings on staying fed and being securely housed. And now, all spent out, they have been added to the numbers seeking help with benefits. (To be eligible for UC an applicant can't have more than £16,000 in savings.)

The rapid spread of the pandemic and the economic lockdown meant no job was safe.

After the 2008 credit crunch it took 12 years to get Britain working and saving again. Overnight people who had got used to earning a wage were, through no fault of their own, back on the scrapheap. Factory output slumped, restaurants and pubs closed, and anyone in the gig economy discovered they could no longer make a sustainable living.

But that wasn't the end of it: those living in poverty-stricken communities found they were more vulnerable to the extreme hardship being wrought by the pandemic.

We know the coronavirus has killed more poor people than rich people. At the time of writing, death rates are more than twice as high in the poorest parts of the country than they are in the richest, according to data from the Office for National Statistics (ONS).[1] While people in low skilled jobs are four times more likely to die from the disease than professionals.[2]

But the UK government's most urgent concern has been the health of the economy.

The Treasury has committed to borrowing £300–£500 billion to keep the economy afloat, with the bulk of the money being diverted to business rescue packages. In addition, a third of the UK work force has been subsidised, costing about £14 billion a month or £80 billion by the end of 2020.

Under the furloughing scheme 8 million people were kept on until the government subsidies ran out and then employers cynically started culling those they already knew they were going to make redundant. Furloughing turned out to be a national time-and-motion study which informed bosses how few employees they needed to run their businesses. Millions of workers disgorged from the hospitality and leisure industries were the first to join the dole queues.

Neither were the highly remunerated and once highly valued white-collar professionals and technocrats keeping their jobs, many of whom were being viewed as surplus to requirements. This time it was the nurses, the binmen and the supermarket shelf fillers who were the 'key workers', the indispensable lifeblood of the nation. Nevertheless, the government still refused to increase the salaries of these traditionally low-paid jobs. Nurses, hailed as the heroes of the pandemic and for whom the government exhorted us all to leave our homes to put our hands together in a show of national appreciation, felt particularly badly treated. Many of them were furious when the Chancellor announced paltry wage rises for some selected public sector workers but left *them* out. Given that there were already 40,000 unfilled nursing jobs it didn't make much economic sense. At the end of 2019 a Royal College of Nursing survey showed that 27 percent of nurses were thinking of giving up. As we saw in Chapter 3 that figure has risen to 70 percent during the pandemic.[3]

But what was true before the coronavirus recession, that some workers are more equal than others, was even more evident when the government oversaw an economic life-support system that treated Britain's richest tycoons to some very generous handouts. Among those first out of the blocks to stake their claim for free taxpayers' cash were some very familiar faces: Richard Branson, Mike Ashley and Philip Green announced their bids for state support even in the teeth of an angry public backlash.

They weren't alone. The *Sunday Times* identified at least sixty-three well-known capitalists who had a significant financial stake in companies which furloughed their staff. (The true figure is likely to be much higher because there is no public list of furloughed companies, and many claims made by the very rich and famous will have gone unreported.) The most prominent was Sir Jim Ratcliffe, a tax exile in Monaco and top of the 2017–18 rich list with a fortune worth £12.15 billion. Ratcliffe requested an emergency government-funded loan of approximately £500 million to bail out his Petroineos business – a joint venture with state-owned PetroChina. Ratcliffe also co-owns the luxury Pig hotel chain, which duly furloughed most of its staff.

The 2018–19 *Sunday Times* wealth winners, Gopi and Sri Hinduja, saw their £22 billion tumble by £6 billion in 2020, a blow that was cushioned by furloughing some of their 360 employees at Optare, their North Yorkshire-based bus-making firm.

Another major beneficiary of the furlough state-subsidy scheme was the Brexiteering hospitality entrepreneur Tim Martin, owner of the Wetherspoons pub chain. Worth £311 million, Martin told his staff to go and get work in a supermarket during the pandemic.

The Weston family – with some £10.53 billion and owners of Selfridges, Fortnum & Mason, Primark and Heal's – rose from

number thirteen to eight in the *Sunday Times* 2020 rich list. They
offloaded tens of thousands of staff on to the taxpayers' payroll.

Sir Henry Keswick is an old friend of David Cameron and
long-standing donor to the Conservative Party whose travel
and hospitality fortune alone was valued at £6.85 billion. The
Keswick family own and run the luxury hotel group Mandarin
Oriental, incorporated in the tax haven of Bermuda, which
not only furloughed its work force but reduced wages and
told staff to take unpaid leave.

For the past three decades the purpose of the *Sunday Times*
rich list has 'been to record that the rich have been getting
richer'. But as the economy dived into an enforced recession
Britain's super-rich saw £54 billion wiped off their combined
wealth in just 2 months.

As we have all witnessed, the pandemic has exposed how
these buccaneers of the 'free market' are more than happy to
take advantage of whatever financial aid package is available.
And who can blame them? Capitalism is a blunt instrument
that imposes financial obligations upon corporations and
shareholders to ensure that they maximise their profits whatever
the ethical cost. The maxim 'profits are private, losses public' was
never more appropriate.

But more egregious crimes of capitalism were to follow. In
the desperate scramble to buy up enough personal protective
equipment (PPE), ministers side-stepped the usual tendering
rules and handed £18 billion of taxpayers' cash to companies,
a number of which had links to individuals in government
and little or no experience of producing PPE.[4]

As the markets plummeted the hedge funds and equity
traders started to circle. By betting on the falling prices, controversial hedge fund manager Crispin Odey was reported to

have profited by £110 million.[5] He made a similar gamble in the wake of Brexit when shares and stocks also took a tumble – and won.

While millions of workers stayed indoors and prepared to cut their cloth according to their essential needs the super-wealthy took to their private jets to escape to their tropical island boltholes. The 'ordinary rich' left the cities for the comfort of their rural retreats. (Who knew that there are 5 million second-home owners in the UK?) The government stirred up further resentment by offering to lift the strict quarantine rules for City executives, bankers and traders who claimed *Corporate UK* would suffer if they had to stay at home for a fortnight following an international 'business' trip.[6]

Meanwhile the rest of Britain locked down and trusted in their employers to keep them on the payroll. Thousands didn't. One of the most haunting images of this crisis of capitalism were pictures of the sacked staff of Britannia Hotels being evicted from their accommodation in the Scottish Highlands. At the same time the newspapers were full of outraged reports of wealthy businessmen buying up desperately needed venti-lators or paying thousands of pounds for private virus tests.

In America senators were even caught secretly offloading their stocks and shares while misleading the American public about how severely the pandemic would impact on the economy. In the UK companies like Tesco took full advan-tage of the run on toilet paper by paying generous dividends to their investors who got rich on the back of the economic paralysis. And the banks, who were bailed out so generously by the state in 2008, had no hesitation in whacking up interest rates for people now desperate to borrow to keep their families fed and their businesses afloat.

Recessions have always hit the poorest hardest and barely touched the wealthy at all. But this time the economic shock was not caused by a run on a bank or a collapse in oil prices. The 2020 pandemic led to a managed economic slowdown which, unlike any other recession before it, allowed the government to make calculated choices about who was expendable and whose lives really matter.

Since the coronavirus began ravaging the economy the inequities of capitalism are plain to see.[7] In the first 3 months of the lockdown one-third of lower-paid employees lost jobs or were furloughed, compared with only one-tenth of top earners.[8] Astonishingly, throughout the pandemic highly paid executives have mostly kept their perks and bonuses.[9] It was always likely that the furloughed staff were at risk of redundancy as soon as the government began to withdraw its support.

But it has been the struggling younger workers, those under twenty-five, who have been truly hit the hardest. Large numbers of young people are employed in the sectors which were most severely affected by the lockdown: leisure, retail and hospitality. One in three young people have been furloughed or lost their jobs completely, and more than one in three have had their pay reduced since the crisis started.[10]

And as the recession has bitten deeper, the casualties have become those already at the bottom of the heap – the unemployed, the sick, the single parents and even the kids on free school meals.

The paltry emergency boost to UC, tax credits and housing support on 20 March 2020 increased incomes of families in the poorest quarter by just 5 percent on average.[11] But even this pitiful increase didn't extend to Statutory Sick Pay, leaving the worse-off struggling to survive on £96 a week. And 2 million part-time workers who earn under £120 a week got nothing at all. It was a policy which left the worse-off workers in the invidious position of having to choose between health and hardship.

The meanness of the state's help for those on benefits is in sharp contrast to the generous income protection provided under the Job Retention Scheme. The median fall in disposable income among those who have been furloughed is just 9 percent, but that figure is 47 percent when people lose their jobs and have to rely on UC. This means that workers who were made redundant as furloughing was cut faced life-changing falls in income.[12]

The government's economic response to the coronavirus has been the introduction of a raft of policies which mirror capitalism's discrimination of the poor. Some actions, like the wave of redundancies following the furloughing scheme and the millions more households relying on UC, are clear to see. But there have been indirect consequences that will take longer to play out.

While most of us were told to stay at home to fight the coronavirus, many low-paid key workers in hospitals, supermarkets and other workplaces have risked their health to keep the economy running.[13] Only time will tell if the government will honour pledges to 'level up' the wages of those doing essential jobs and whether it will continue to devote resources to solving chronic social ills such as homelessness.

One of the disguised blessings of our economic recession has been the knock-on benefit to the environment. For the first time in a century industrial output across the world almost stopped. (Citizens of the polluted cities of Delhi and Beijing could see the sky again.) But history suggests politicians have short memories once the first green shoots of an economic recovery start to appear.

In 1918–19 during the Spanish global flu pandemic carbon emissions also fell by 14 percent when industrial production and consumption slowed down dramatically. But 1 year later, after the virus had wiped out 20 million people, production and pollution rose by 16 percent by 1920. 'Back then we were on the upswing. We were seeing ever faster population growth worldwide; back then a pandemic could not slow us down for long', says Danny Dorling, the Oxford geography academic and author of *Slowdown: The End of the Great Acceleration – and Why It's Good for the Planet, the Economy, and Our Lives.*[14]

Politicians also made rash promises when they faced similar choices after the credit crunch of 2008. But in the 12 years separating the two recessions, the super-rich have continued to grow their wealth while tens of millions of workers have suffered a decade of savage austerity to pay for the bailout of the banks and the corporations. This time governments must learn the lessons of the failed, short-termism remedies of the past and use the pandemic to improve the prospects for all of us – not just for the wealthy few.

20

ENRICHING OUR SOCIETY

HOW WE ALL GET RICH

We have been getting richer by roughly 1.5 percent[1] every year since the Industrial Revolution began in 1750. Our gross domestic product (GDP), the measure of the country's economic activity, may have faltered by way of recession and war but its overall trajectory continues skywards. Even now our virus-ravaged economy is starting to climb back to growth. Each generation produces and consumes more goods than the last and is on average one-third better off by GDP. The UK is the fifth biggest economy in the world where, before the pandemic struck, more people were in work since records began. Any day now Boris Johnson will tell us 'we have never had it so good'.

So why doesn't it feel that way? Why are so many people trapped at the bottom of the heap struggling to earn a living? To answer these questions we must first recognise seven paradoxes which paint a complex and complicating picture of our prosperity:

- The economy may be growing in the long term but productivity, or the rate of economic output, has stalled to levels not seen for 250 years.[2]
- We are the fifth largest economy based on GDP but our wealth is spread so unevenly among the population that we

are only the twenty-ninth richest country in the world per capita.[3]

- Since 1971 the proportion of the population in employment has been steadily growing but today one in five of us (14 million) is living and working in relative poverty,[4] and since 2000 the number of people living in deep poverty has nearly doubled (2.8–4.5 million).[5]

- Record numbers of women have jobs[6] while the number of men employed has fallen by 12 percent since 1971,[7] yet the UK is ranked fifty-eighth in the world in terms of economic gender equality.[8]

- The curb on migrant workers from the EU will mean British workers will have to fill the hundreds of thousands of vacancies in care homes, hospitals and hotels. But wages have stagnated to pre-2008 levels.

- More new homes (241,130) were built in 2019[9] than at any time since 1990, yet in the same year homeless deaths were reported to have hit record levels rising from just over 400 deaths in 2013 to 778.[10]

- For the first time in our history life expectancy has started to fall at the same time that we are experiencing the greatest medical breakthroughs of our age. One reason for this might be that we have reached peak wealth and are starting to kill ourselves through overconsumption (obesity leading to heart disease, for example) as well as drug and alcohol abuse.[11]

So despite this superficial picture of inexorable global economic growth, capitalism is facing profound, complex and conflicting challenges. The biggest challenge is that the system is simply not paying out enough money to enough people who need it while still making rich people even richer. Perhaps it always did. But we are now at a critical point in our economic evolution where making enough money to improve the quality of our lives is neither attainable nor even credible for the majority. This is not about the failure of some kind of 'American dream' but more a betrayal of the sense of British fair play and a breach of capitalism's contract which promises that hard work always pays off.

The UK is not uniquely afflicted by these socioeconomic paradoxes. Wealth inequality in America has reached dystopian proportions, productivity in Germany has dipped to levels last seen in the days of the Weimar Republic and living standards in France have caused its citizens to don *gilets jaunes* and return to the barricades. In Denmark growth is so low that its banks have launched the world's first negative interest rates so that borrowers are being paid to take on debt.[12]

Nevertheless, there is a narrow, thriving class of super-rich who are getting richer. Between 2009 and 2019 the number of billionaires in the UK doubled and in that time the wealth of those billionaires has *more* than doubled.

The richest 1 percent of people in the UK own the same wealth as 80 percent of the population – 53 million people. And the concentration of this wealth is so great that the five richest families own more wealth than 13 million people.[13] The French economist Thomas Piketty describes this super-wealthy elite as the return of the aristocracy, reliant on inherited wealth which generates income at a much greater rate than that achieved by the sluggish growth of the world economies.

But these are not the indolent, decadent aristocracy of eighteenth-century Paris. The super-rich of today are toiling harder than ever to keep hold of their wealth. Daniel Markovits, in his book *The Meritocracy Trap: How America's Foundational Myth Feeds Inequality, Dismantles the Middle Class, and Devours the Elite*, says that the richest members of society are working an average of 12 more hours per week than middle-class workers, the equivalent of 1.5 additional workdays.[14] Nearly two-thirds of high-earning individuals work over 50 hours a week, more than a third work over 60 hours a week, and 10 percent work a minimum of 80 hours a week.[15] There may be a few oligarch types and pampered tycoons who are decadently swinging the lead while squandering their fortunes, but those are the exceptions, the mirage in the economy that spur us on to follow our impossible dreams of fabulous wealth and idle living.

Does it matter that a narrow section of society is being disproportionately enriched? It may not feel fair, but is it bad for Britain? This question has not been properly addressed by left-wing economists who decry economic inequality for creating unequal societies but don't spell out the effects of this iniquity. Prosperity is by its nature a relative condition. When we compare our economic lives to those of our grandparents we are all better off. More people have roofs over their heads, we have more modern conveniences, enjoy more luxuries and we have access to a far superior health service. So who cares if a few thousand people have a lot more of all this than the average person? As Peter Mandelson once said, shouldn't we all be 'intensely relaxed about people getting filthy rich'?

To identify the harm of extreme inequality to the overall economy it is necessary to appreciate the structural and socio-economic changes to the work force since the end of the Second World War. The problem no longer comes from the bottom of society but from the middle. In 1971, when my father-in-law went to watch the FA Cup Final at Wembley, middle-class workers made up 32 percent of the total work force. By 2000 the UK was equally split[16] between working-class and middle-class households. But just 20 years later nearly two-thirds of families in the UK have gravitated to the middle-income class. In France, Hungary, Holland, Czech Republic, Japan and Israel the proportion is touching 70 percent.[17] More than half of the global population is middle class by income.[18] We are all middle class now, or will be soon.

This is a significant change because capitalism is built on the aspiration of the middle classes.

The encapsulating definition of middle-class ambition used to be comfortable living, but instead they have become the 'squeezed middle' or as one British prime minister famously declared the 'just about managing'. Once the maths becomes impossible and people can see that no matter how hard they work they may never own their own home, holiday abroad, buy a new car and comfortably retire, aren't they entitled to ask what they are working for? A similar despondency afflicts large numbers of the working rich who are trapped in a long-hours office culture, deprived of family association and time spent enjoying the fruits of their wealth. And as we have seen, many of the most vulnerable members of society are being driven to despair by the precarity of their situation. At the bottom of the pile more than a fifth of the population live on incomes below the poverty line, even though most of these households have members in work. Nearly one in three children are being brought up in poverty, and austerity and restrictions on benefits means more and more citizens, including nurses and police officers, are making use of food banks. The economic impact of the coronavirus has dragged millions more into destitution.

Our country is producing more wealth but the economy is not distributing it fairly. For the younger generations, whom the nation relies on to pay for the retirement of the coming generations, the economic future looks particularly bleak and ergo particularly bleak for everybody else too.

Danny Dorling, the Oxford professor of geography who has led the way in the investigation of inequality in Britain, says no other EU/OECD (Organisation for Economic Co-operation and Development) country is as unequal as the UK.[19] Regional and social divisions in society are set to become even more extreme than they are at present. Our cities are getting richer and their environs are being left behind.[20] In the new societies of tomorrow the elites will own all the shelter, all the food and all the water.

A successful society requires a majority of its citizens to believe they have a realistic chance of benefiting from social mobility. But recent research has shown that people on low incomes increasingly believe the economy is rigged against them.[21] It turns out that this is a suspicion supported by a harsh reality: children born into very disadvantaged communities rarely escape them – no matter how well they do at school.[22]

And as more and more citizens give up on creating a more profitable society, communities start to crumble.

Given the accelerating climate emergency we must get to grips with the paradoxes of modern capitalism[23] and find a new economic model that tackles the problems confronting our overheating planet. Otherwise, the rules that govern the societies of the future will be determined by a chaotic 'gold rush' for ever-diminishing resources.

Time is running out for capitalism, or more accurately *capitalism* is running out of time.

The balance of the world's wealth is shifting. Soon we will be unable to dictate the terms of our own terminal decline. Key decisions will no longer be ours to take. By 2034 the global economy may be $200 trillion.[24] Such a world is very different from the one we see today. It will be significantly wealthier, with global per-capita incomes averaging $21,300 as compared with $8,000 today. The economic centre of gravity will have tilted towards Asia, which today accounts for 34 percent of global activity but by 2034 could account for 57 percent of global output.[25] What won't have changed will be the structural inequalities of future capitalist societies.

Capitalism may not be broken, it may just require a full service and a reconfiguration.

But how do we fix our own economic system so that everyone has a chance; how do we upgrade to capitalism 2.0? We will need to tackle both the economic and cultural barriers holding back a fairer distribution of wealth and happiness.

The coronavirus has gifted the world a chance to recalibrate our imbalanced economies. Courtesy of the pandemic we now know how many 'bullshit jobs' there are, how many pointless business journeys we take every year, how so little of the working week needs to take place in an office and how much valueless and unnecessary product we produce.

In some respects we have reached the same pivotal moment we did in the 1970s which marked the collapse of the post-war system of fixed exchange rates, capital controls and wage policies, which were perceived to have led to uncontrollable inflation.

In 1974 the cost of a barrel of oil rose by 400 percent when oil producers imposed oil embargos, plunging the world into an energy crisis. Such a sharp shock to basic living standards in the West ushered in the market-dominated economic thinking that underpinned the governments of Margaret Thatcher and Ronald Reagan who brought in tax cuts, interest rate rises and an economic dogma that put profit and shareholder value above everything else.

While the raging inflation of the 1970s and the financial crisis 50 years later were perceived as problems integral to the workings of the global economy, the coronavirus crisis is a managed economic slowdown brought about by reduced consumption. For example, airlines were deliberately grounded and oil prices actually dropped to below zero as producers were forced to respond to a collapse in demand.

World economies paused and governments started to collect their thoughts and look for new ideas to breathe life back into an economic system that no longer seemed capable of answering new questions being asked of it. The fiscal and monetary radicalism deployed by the government in response to the coronavirus crisis has meant economic policy is no longer so easily captured by the ideologies of the left or the right.

On 1 June 2020 Britain's most powerful business leaders wrote a letter to Boris Johnson setting out an economic recovery plan that would create a fairer economy for all while also aligning the UK with climate goals. Nearly 200 chief executives – from companies including HSBC, National Grid, Heathrow Airport, Aviva, Lloyds Banking Group and BP's UK business – called on the prime minister to 'deliver a clean, just recovery'.[26] These captains of industry and commerce said they wanted a recovery that 'creates quality employment' and helps to build 'a more sustainable, inclusive and resilient UK economy for the future'.

Have the City moguls and industrial tycoons ever proposed such action against the very system that made them so prosperous?

To achieve these ambitious goals Britain will have to make radical changes to a range of economic policies, even more radical than those the business leaders recognised in their letter. These reforms must address the seven socioeconomic paradoxes I have identified. But they must also tackle structural socioeconomic ills such as growing intergenerational inequality, falling social mobility and the market dominance of the new online and social media corporate giants.

All this can be achieved by following three distinct programmes of reform: a more efficient and progressive taxation system; the introduction of a universal basic income; and a New Green Deal to create more sustainable jobs while also contributing to the arrest of climate change.

A fairer taxation system must deliver more money to more people. This will require new land and inheritance taxes to block wealth being passed from ancestral hegemony to ancestral hegemony. The focus must be on the transfer of assets, because the one thing we have learned from the 2008 crisis is that given enough time, the depleted wealth of the super-rich dynasties will always bounce back.

This is because newly printed money being pumped into the economy by the Bank of England to keep the economy afloat gravitates to the already wealthy. Within 10 years from mid-2008 the super-rich, thanks to their indestructible assets, were back in boom times. The price of gold had trebled, the value of UK stocks doubled and house prices went off the scale. This all happened despite persistent weaknesses in our economy. As governments borrow even more cash to buy their way out of the COVID-19 recession there is every reason to believe that history will repeat itself.

So new inheritance taxes must break the processional transfer of wealth from one wealthy generation to another. We must end the situation where fewer than 5 percent of the 588,000 deaths each year in the UK attract inheritance tax. And new laws must also stop the wealthy gifting their tax-free inheritances to their families before they die. At the same time tougher capital gains taxes must be imposed on property owners who sell homes which have gone up in value. In these ways we can reconcile the most critical paradox of being the world's fifth largest economy but the twenty-ninth in terms of fair distribution of national wealth.[27]

Targeted taxes will also be needed to break down the new monopolies of our internet and social media age. As we have seen in earlier chapters, the tech giants – Google, Facebook, Microsoft and Amazon – have insidiously risen to dominate their markets at the expense of their online users, customers and shoppers.

The banks too have been allowed to act together to stifle competition so they can pick the pockets of life's strugglers. They have stolen billions of pounds from us in the form of payment protection insurance, hidden overdraft fees and extortionate credit card charges.[28]

As John Kenneth Galbraith prophetically identified in his prequel to *The Affluent Society*, *American Capitalism: The Concept of Countervailing Power* (1952), these 'imperfections' undermine the free markets and work against public interest. Actually he went further, arguing what should really matter is the countervailing power of other vested interests including suppliers, customers and trade unions.[29]

We must build a consensus to tackle the old and new monopolies and support the 'countervailing powers' of the twenty-first century. This will mean imposing tough residency-based taxes and empowering regulators to take on the forces of anti-competitiveness that hold back the customer and the worker. This isn't 'big brother' interference in the liberal economy, this is harnessing the power of the markets to serve the greater good.

We have of course been here before in the Great Depression of the 1930s, triggered by the Wall Street Crash.[30] The solution then was a New Deal, an economic recovery plan which dismantled the international financial system known as the 'gold standard' and brought about unprecedented government-backed programmes for relief, recovery and reform.

The world is facing just as grave a threat to the global economy today – perhaps even graver, because this time we are not only being battered by raging debts, sluggish growth, negative interest rates and falling productivity but we must also meet the challenge of a climate-change emergency while confronting the constant threat of renewed outbreaks of the coronavirus. Fortunately there already exists a package of reforms purposely designed to tackle this unique pending catastrophe.

The Green New Deal, just like the New Deal, has been conceived in America. Its twin purpose is to build a more equal society while neutralising the threat of climate change. Although its origins are in American politics – championed by Alexandria Ocasio-Cortez, the youngest woman to be elected to the House of Representatives and widely tipped to be a presidential candidate in 2024 – it has been taken up all over the world.

In the UK it has been adopted by groups of cross-party politicians, economists and media commentators, including the Green Deal Group[31] and the New Economics Foundation.[32] Those cheerleading for a Green New Deal come from a diverse range of political and academic backgrounds. They include the London mayor, Sadiq Khan, and the conservative mayor of the West Midlands, Andy Street, as well as fair tax campaigner Richard Murphy and the political economist Ann Pettifor. The movement's principal aim is to bring down carbon emissions such that by 2030, 100 percent of power is generated through clean, renewable and zero-emission energy sources.[33] Thirty million energy-sustainable and affordable homes will be built or old ones made green. In the process of achieving a green-based economy millions of new jobs will be created. These green jobs will offer timely and well-paid employment to the millions of workers who have become economic casualties of the coronavirus recession.

This may sound revolutionary but it represents a return to the popular post-war economic movements and philosophies espoused by economists such as Galbraith. These in turn were influenced by philosophers[34] like Bertrand Russell whose seminal essay, *In Praise of Idleness*, set out the foundations for a programme of reform where instead of punishing people for being out of work they would be supported with living salaries. Galbraith and Russell argued that society would function more efficiently if the working week was reduced and the jobless were compensated for their idleness rather than sanctioned as they are today under our social benefits system. They were the forefathers of the furloughed economy and the universal basic wage.

But the high ideal of letting people earn a comfortable living while being unemployed is anathema to the political class of today. They argue that it stands to reason if you pay people to be idle then they will stop making a contribution to society. It might sound counter-intuitive, but this is not what has happened in countries which have experimented with a universal basic income system. When Canada paid a community in Manitoba a free wage in the 1970s, everybody benefited.[35] In Finland the universal basic income scheme has been running since 2017. Preliminary findings from the Finnish study are encouraging: 2,000 unemployed people across Finland were paid a tax-free income of 560 euros a month. There were no other conditions to receiving the payment. After 2 years the levels of unemployment had hardly changed[36] but there was a huge difference to the participants' sense of happiness and well-being: fifty-five percent who took part said their state of health was good or very good, while only 46 percent of the 173,000 control group of benefit recipients were able to say the same. And there were other unseen advantages. Overnight the work done by unpaid carers and full-time parents was now financially rewarded, while the bill for maintaining a complex benefits system was slashed.

Other countries have followed suit. Three provinces in the Netherlands have now implemented basic income pilots, and there are much larger trials taking place in India and Kenya. In the UK, councils in Edinburgh, Glasgow and Fife have advanced plans for similar schemes. The idea has even been turned into a format for commercial television.

In 2017 Channel 5's *Great British Benefits Handout* was an experiment that paid families a lump sum of £26,000. Studies show that if you give people a lot of money to turn their lives around and match it with training and financial literacy education, you can recoup millions in the long term. As we have seen, this means the community and the country benefit through savings in ongoing benefit support, taxes paid and reduced crime. When the Channel 5 series was first screened many people prophesied financial disaster within the year (the period for which the money was supposed to last). Many viewers expected the families who took part to simply blow the cash. But instead it turned out that there was a much stronger desire to try to protect their windfall and each family was back in work before the end of the year.

There would be other benefits to society too. A universal basic income could overnight eradicate in-work poverty, confront dangerously high obesity levels and reverse growing child poverty.

If we help more young people by paying them a 'starting life' wage, supported by free access to lifelong further education, we would also be striking a blow against the exploitation of poverty by crime gangs including the 'county lines' evil drugs trade which preys on impoverished communities. Such a system would also save billions of pounds in benefits fraud, because if everyone is being paid relatively similar free wages it would be impossible to cheat the benefits system.

No doubt there will still be a few liggers who take advantage of the new system. But are they any worse than the corporate Luddites sitting on fortunes and holding back the economy? Or more of a scourge on society than insider traders, hedge fund asset strippers and tax haven money launderers? And do we really have a choice at this stage?

The reforms needed to create a fairer society can rebalance the economy of Britain. But they can only succeed by fostering corresponding cultural changes in tune with a new legal framework. If a government is going to embark on such a radical reform agenda of a universal basic wage, higher wealth taxes and tough green measures, then it must justify this to the electorate. So we must strive for a consensus that acknowledges other ways of measuring and valuing economic growth and non-financial contributions to our society. In one crucial respect the seismic economic reforms brought about by the coronavirus have helped lay the groundwork. Politicians of all political hues have been forced to abandon the economic dogmas of prudent and balanced budgets in favour of magic money trees.

Today it is much easier to argue that value has become too closely associated with price and profit. So when economists measure the size and growth of a country's economic output, the final figure is distorted by shareholder self-interest or 'value' controlled by private equity and venture capital firms. It is better to distinguish between value creation and value extraction so that more emphasis is placed on the first. The measure of real value is what an economy creates, not how many individuals or private entities are getting rich on the back of other people's industry.

The Italian-American economist Mariana Mazzucato argues that GDP needs to differentiate between unproductive and pro-ductive 'earned income'. She says that the way GDP is evaluated today 'justifies excessive inequalities of income and wealth and turns value extraction into value creation'.[37] We can go further still and reward the unseen contributions and contributors to the economy. Because under capitalism 1.0 the more obviously your work directly benefits other people the less you are likely to get paid. So why not, for example, increase the income tax allowance of volunteers who give their time freely to charities?

A much more useful measure of a country's wealth is the Genuine Progress Indicator,[38] which attempts to identify environmental and social costs and benefits as well as valuing household and volunteer work. In 2019 the estimated value of the UK voluntary sector was £79 billion.[39] Unpaid carers have been estimated to save the taxpayer up to £119 billion, which is more than the NHS budget and equivalent to nearly 9 percent of the entire value of the UK economy.[40] Perhaps the greatest lesson of the pandemic is our shameful failure in not recognising the worth of all our key workers. Unpaid carers have as much right to have their value to society quantified as highly paid bankers do. At the same time we must also properly raise the wages of all those who look after us in times of emergency – nurses, firemen and police officers. We now have the perfect chance to reward Britain's essential workers and first responders with more generous pay and reverse the post-recession trend of stagnating wages. And remember fairer pay is not just good for society it also makes economic sense: if we pay nurses generously, they won't keep leaving the NHS, saving millions of pounds in training new ones.

Separately we will have to place more emphasis on the well-being of the population. After all, what is the purpose of having a growing economy serving an unhappy nation? We have already discovered that happy workers tend to work harder and make other valuable, unseen and unmeasured contributions to society.

In 2010 David Cameron accepted the need to focus on more than a crude GDP measurement of national wealth. The UK now publishes a national well-being survey by the ONS that measures factors such as people's self-reported happiness and anxiety levels, their life satisfaction on a scale from 1 to 10 and the rate at which they feel that what they do with their lives is worthwhile. This needs to be included in the basket of measurements of the nation's overall economic health, alongside the price of smartphones and toilet paper.

Some are even challenging the conventional wisdom that growth is by definition a good thing, arguing you cannot have continuing GDP growth and continuing life on this planet. The economist Ann Pettifor says: 'We have commoditised and monetised almost everything. We need to stop growing, we need to extract less from the earth'. To ask a country to give up on economic growth may be asking too much. But we must find economic inhibitors to help wean us off our over-consumption of the earth's resources.

So if we are largely agreed that we must stick with the basic model of capitalism, then we must ensure the work force has vested interest in the economy, confident it will improve their life circumstances. In other words, workers need to know that they have at least a chance of getting rich and that their elected leaders support this aspiration for all citizens. A flatter system for the distribution of riches so that more people are making more money will improve the economic and mental health of the whole country. Wage and working incentives would help reconcile the paradox of an ever-growing economy and stalling productivity. They may even help attract a home-grown work force of well-paid workers to take on the jobs once filled by EU employees. Perhaps most surprisingly of all it may also improve the lives of the 1 percent who hold disproportionate wealth. A study carried out in America found that money makes very wealthy people spiritually poorer.[41]

In *The Spirit Level: Why More Equal Societies Almost Always Do Better* authors Richard G. Wilkinson and Kate Pickett set out to examine why more unequal societies are unhappier places to live. They discovered that inequality leads to social and status anxiety – for everyone. It doesn't matter that we have all that we need if our friends or neighbours live in bigger houses and send their children to fee-paying schools.

Social disparity stokes feelings of envy and dissatisfaction. We become unhappier with what we have because, in comparison, it never feels like enough.

> What matters in rich countries may not be your actual income level and living standard but how you compare to other people in the same society. What matters is if you are doing better or worse than other people and where you are in the pecking order.[42]

Being rich has always been crudely analogous to being successful. Ineluctably, not everyone can be rich and successful; otherwise, neither term means anything. The current system has tended to create far more losers than winners rather than fairly rationing out success. But isn't it better, more rewarding for all of society, to inculcate a culture in which everyone can claim to feel rich? A universal basic income allows everyone to choose how they want to be rich, whether through the capitalist system or through other less directly profitable activity.

There is another reason why we need to recalibrate capitalism. Our democratic system has been badly damaged by Brexit and the coronavirus. Democracy relies on the confidence and trust of the electorate. In the 2019 general election, 55 million adults had the right to vote. But only 47.5 million were *registered* to vote, of whom 31.9 million actually voted. This means nearly 23 million (41.8 percent) took no part in choosing a government. (Only one in five of the population actually voted for Boris Johnson's government.) In the 1950s, when Galbraith was critiquing the affluent societies of the West, turnout in the UK was 84 percent and it remained high until the recession of 1992 when it plummeted to under 60 percent.

One way to interpret this is that more people today have a fatalistic attachment to the system of government. They feel it doesn't matter whether they cast their vote or not because they don't benefit either way. There is a correlation between hard times and low turnout. But there is an even greater link between poverty and political disengagement. People in the top 10 percent of the income distribution are significantly more trusting of government and politicians[43] than those in the bottom 20 percent. Poverty brings disenfranchisement when those living unstable lives are removed or remove themselves from official electoral registers.

In America nearly half the population take no part in elections.[44] (Even though there was a record turnout in 2020, 81 million eligible voters stayed away.) Switzerland has a turnout of just 36 percent. In 2016 Australia experienced the lowest recorded turnout since the introduction of compulsory voting in the 1920s.[45] In the UK one in three people don't vote. One of the most decisive reasons for not voting in the UK is the sense that there is no social or economic mobility.[46] For so many people these structural inequalities mean the good things in life will simply pass them by. They will remain outsiders looking in on better lives. Millions more won't even know what they are missing out on. And for them ignorance is far from bliss.

That is perhaps the single greatest issue the country faces today, the one which drives politics, which in turn drives our national responses to all kinds of environmental and societal ills. If we want to rebuild trust in our governments and our democracy, people must feel they have a financial stake in society. The strivers, grafters and strugglers must all believe they can get rich.

ACKNOWLEDGEMENTS

I am grateful to everyone who generously shared their expertise and experiences in the research for this book: from the economists who helped explain the theories of capitalism to those on the breadline who gave voice to its iniquities.

Special thanks to Cecilia Stein, Alex Christofi, Kate Bland, Paul Nash, Danny Dorling, Francis Green, Piers Blofeld, Father Kevin Dring, Lind, Stan, Walt, everyone at Oneworld and all those who can't be named.

NOTES

All links were correct at the time of writing and were last accessed in November 2020.

Introduction: The Road to Wembley

1 www.thefa.com/news/2017/apr/25/the-emirates-fa-cup-final-details-250417

2 www.officialdata.org/uk/inflation/1971?endYear=2017&amount=1

3 In 2019 that £1 was worth £14.24; www.bankofengland.co.uk/monetary-policy/inflation/inflation-calculator

4 www.in2013dollars.com/uk/inflation/1971?endYear=2018&amount=1

5 www.bankofengland.co.uk/monetary-policy/inflation/inflation-calculator

6 www.standard.co.uk/go/london/bars/cheapest-pint-beer-london-pubs-a4004121.html

7 www.90min.com/posts/4685413-bayern-fans-revolt-inside-emirates-stadium-over-ticket-prices-during-their-5-1-win-over-arsenal?fbclid=IwAR0bhJ5BltBYvy9bpxG9TVrv2RwpCztjIiZDdII_qP3CmQ8JkAktbDljafM

8 www.terramedia.co.uk/reference/statistics/cinema/cinema_ticket_prices_1.htm

9 https://landregistry.data.gov.uk/app/ukhpi

10 www.bankofengland.co.uk/monetary-policy/inflation/inflation-
   calculator; www.ons.gov.uk/employmentandlabourmarket/
   peopleinwork/earningsandworkinghours/bulletins/annualsur-
   veyofhoursandearnings/2019; www.ons.gov.uk/economy/
   inflationandpriceindices/bulletins/consumerpriceinflation/july2020;
   www.ons.gov.uk/economy/inflationandpriceindices/bulletins/
   housepriceindex/may2020
11 www.thisismoney.co.uk/money/news/article-7150007/What-life-
   like-1970s-Britain-time-unemployment-low.html
12 Median annual earnings for 2019; www.bankofengland.co.uk/
   monetary-policy/inflation/inflation-calculator; www.ons.gov.uk/
   employmentandlabourmarket/peopleinwork/
   earningsandworkinghours/bulletins/
   annualsurveyofhoursandearnings/2019
13 https://fullfact.org/economy/employment-since-2010-wages
14 www.tuc.org.uk/news/
   workers-still-suffering-longest-pay-squeeze-200-years-says-tuc
15 www.tuc.org.uk/blogs/our-broken-economy-has-locked-millions-
   workers-poverty-heres-how-fix-it
16 www.resolutionfoundation.org/publications/feel-poor-work-more
17 www.centreforcities.org/publication/hidden-unemployment
   -in-uk-cities
18 www.resolutionfoundation.org/app/uploads/2019/11/Feel-poor-
   work-more.pdf
19 Nicholas Crafts and Terence C. Mills, 'Is the UK productivity
   slowdown unprecedented?', *National Institute Economic Review*, Vol.
   251, pp. R47–R53. [Online]. (URL https://doi.org/10.1017/
   nie.2020.6). (Accessed 7 September 2020).
20 www.ons.gov.uk/employmentandlabourmarket/peopleinwork/
   labourproductivity/bulletins/labourproductivity/julytoseptember2019
21 But if we all want to get rich in this country then we have all got to be
   better at being more efficient workers and employers, that is, producing
   more goods in less time. If we don't actually have record employment,
   as the OECD claims, then improving productivity is the only way to
   increase the real, long-term individual prosperity of the UK.

22 www.thersa.org/globalassets/pdfs/reports/rsa_7-portraits-of-modern-work-report.pdf

23 www.bbc.com/news/business-44926447 (2018 Resolution Foundation living standards going backwards)

24 www.trusselltrust.org/news-and-blog/latest-stats

25 www.thesun.co.uk/news/7122204/opinion-stella-creasy-loan-sharks

26 www.theguardian.com/society/2018/nov/16/uk-austerity-has-inflicted-great-misery-on-citizens-un-says; www.theguardian.com/politics/2019/may/22/un-report-compares-tory-welfare-reforms-to-creation-of-workhouses; www.theguardian.com/politics/2019/may/22/amber-rudd-to-lodge-complaint-over-un-austerity-report

27 www.ifs.org.uk/inequality/wp-content/uploads/2019/05/The-IFS-Deaton-Review-launch.pdf (IFS stats)

28 www.ifs.org.uk/uploads/BN254-Characteristics-and-Incomes-Of-The-Top-1%25.pdf; Alvaredo, F., Atkinson, A.B., Piketty, T., *et al.*, Country Data from the World Wealth and Income Database, 2019. Available at: www.wid.world. (Accessed 28 January 2019).

29 www.suttontrust.com/wp-content/uploads/2020/01/Pulling-Away-1.pdf

30 Interview with the author, January 2020

31 www.theguardian.com/business/2015/mar/06/johns-davids-and-ians-outnumber-female-chief-executives-in-ftse-100

32 http://highpaycentre.org/blog/high-pay-day-2020-scope-for-fairer-pay-and-lower-inequality-remains-conside

33 https://academic.oup.com/ereh/article/17/1/1/493819; http://victorian-era.org/the-victorian-era-wages-salary-earnings.html; www.victorianweb.org/economics/wages2.html

34 www.ons.gov.uk/peoplepopulationandcommunity/personalandhouseholdfinances/incomeandwealth/bulletins/totalwealthingreatbritain/april2016tomarch2018

35 www.theguardian.com/news/2019/sep/09/inequality-is-it-rising-and-can-we-reverse-it

36 www.suttontrust.com/wp-content/uploads/2020/01/Pulling-Away-1.pdf

37 www.oecd-ilibrary.org/sites/689afed1-en/index.html?itemId=/
    content/publication/689afed1-en&mimeType=text/html
38 www.suttontrust.com/wp-content/uploads/2020/01/Pulling-
    Away-1.pdf
39 www.resolutionfoundation.org/publications/who-owns-all-the-pie;
    www.bbc.co.uk/news/uk-48759591
40 www.resolutionfoundation.org/publications/who-owns-all-the-pie
41 www.theguardian.com/inequality/2019/may/14/britain-risks-
    heading-to-us-levels-of-inequality-warns-top-economist; www.ifs.
    org.uk/inequality/chapter/briefing-note
42 When capitalised in this book, 'City' refers specifically to the busi-
    nesses, culture and people who derive a living from the financial
    services, exchanges and money markets.
43 www.bbc.co.uk/news/uk-politics-48503170
44 www.prweek.com/article/1671233/
    edelman-trust-barometer-worlds-population-down-capitalism
45 www.vox.com/2019/1/10/18171912/tucker-carlson-fox-news-
    populism-conservatism-trump-gop; www.theguardian.com/
    commentisfree/2019/feb/02/inequality-fox-news-tucker-carlson-
    capitalism?CMP=Share_iOSApp_Othe
46 The ILO used labour income figures from 189 countries between
    2004 and 2017. The latest data are available at: www.ilo.org/global/
    about-the-ilo/newsroom/news/WCMS_712234/lang--en/index.
    htm
47 Adam Smith, *The Theory of Moral Sentiments* (Andrew Millar of
    London and Alexander Kincaid of Edinburgh, 1759).

1 What Is Rich? The Billionaire Who Thinks Everybody is Worth £660,791

1 www.channel4.com/news/factcheck/
   factcheck-council-house-tenants-earn-60000
2 www.ifs.org.uk/publications/14303
3 www.ifs.org.uk/publications/14303

4   www.resolutionfoundation.org/comment/who-owns-britains-13tn-
      wealth; www.bbc.co.uk/news/uk-48759591

5   www.oecd.org/unitedkingdom/Middle-class-
      2019-United-Kingdom.pdf; www.oecd.org/social/
      under-pressure-the-squeezed-middle-class-689afed1-en.htm

6   www.compareyourincome.org

7   https://assets.publishing.service.gov.uk/government/uploads/system/
      uploads/attachment_data/file/752045/impact_on_households_
      distributional_analysis_to_accompany_budget_2018_web.pdf

8   www.gov.uk/tier-1-investor

9   www.ifs.org.uk/publications/14303

10   www.ons.gov.uk/employmentandlabourmarket/
       peopleinwork/earningsandworkinghours/bulletins/
       annualsurveyofhoursandearnings/2019

11   ONS median weekly wage for April 2019 was £585; www.ons.gov.
       uk/employmentandlabourmarket/peopleinwork/
       earningsandworkinghours/bulletins/
       annualsurveyofhoursandearnings/2019

12   www.ifs.org.uk/tools_and_resources/where_do_you_fit_in

13   That is, where differences in household size and composition are
       taken into consideration.

14   www.ons.gov.uk/peoplepopulationandcommunity/
       personalandhouseholdfinances/incomeandwealth/datasets/
       householddisposableincomeandinequality

15   www.resolutionfoundation.org/comment/who-owns-britains-
       13tn-wealth

16   www.fmb.org.uk/about-the-fmb/newsroom/construction-
       apprentices-will-earn-more-than-uni-students

17   www.legalcheek.com/2017/02/
       research-average-barrister-earnings-equate-to-60000-salary

18   www.givingwhatwecan.org/get-involved/how-rich-am-i

19   Calculated from the mean of a basket of nine incomes and salaries,
       given by inter alia HMRC, OECD, HM Treasury and the IFS. Three
       of the nine figures relate to household incomes.

2 Survivors: The Insurance Salesman Who Didn't Leave His Home for 4 Years

1 www.cityam.com/article/
   why-britain-s-housing-market-has-escaped-disasters-1990s

2 https://blog.topsteptrader.com/story-of-george-soros-breaking-
   the-bank-of-england

3 www.theguardian.com/business/2012/sep/13/black-wednesday-
   20-years-pound-erm

4 https://blog.topsteptrader.com/story-of-george-soros-breaking-
   the-bank-of-england

5 www.independent.co.uk/news/uk/politics/record-number-of-
   companies-go-bust-1848117.html

6 www.tuc.org.uk/blogs/our-broken-economy-has-locked-millions-
   workers-poverty-heres-how-fix-it;
   www.ifs.org.uk/publications/13302; www.ons.gov.
   uk/economy/grossdomesticproductgdp/articles/
   the2008recession10yearson/2018-04-30

7 https://esrc.ukri.org/files/news-events-and-publications/
   publications/themed-publications/recession-britain;
   www.economicshelp.org/macroeconomics/economic-growth/
   uk-recession-1991

3 First Responders: The Hungry Nurse Who Ate the Patient's Sandwich

1 www.channel4.com/news/
   food-banks-key-questions-hunger-austerity-welfare-cuts

2 www.youtube.com/watch?v=xK-8n-daMmE; www.mirror.co.uk/
   news/politics/top-tory-sparks-fury-saying-10522606

3 www.rcn.org.uk/get-help/member-support-services/lamplight/
   guide-to-financial-assistance

4 https://fullfact.org/economy/how-many-nurses-are-using-foodbanks

5 www.nursingtimes.net/one-in-five-student-midwives-will-be-left-
   with-10k-debt/5008978.article

www.kingsfund.org.uk/blog/2017/07/
why-we-shouldnt-panic-about-nursing-students-yet

6 www.mirror.co.uk/news/uk-news/
hard-up-nurses-being-forced-9105992

7 www.cashfloat.co.uk/blog/community/more-nurses-apply-for-
payday-loans; www.cashfloat.co.uk/blog/loans-lenders/payday-
loans-for-nurses

8 https://nursingnotes.co.uk/news/workforce/poor-pay-bullying-see-
large-numbers-of-nurses-wanting-leave-profession/

9 https://rcnfoundation.rcn.org.uk/news/covid-19-support-fund

10 www.mirror.co.uk/all-about/sussex-police

11 www.bbc.co.uk/news/uk-22715458; www.fbu.org.uk/
news/2017/11/23/miserable-budget-workers-says-union

12 www.politicshome.com/news/uk/home-affairs/policing/news/
86010/amber-rudd-ridiculed-police-federation-over-foodbank-answer

13 Interviews with the author (October 2019)

14 www.nursinginpractice.com/
nurses-can-only-afford-own-home-3-british-towns-report-finds

15 www.theguardian.com/film/2019/nov/28/the-dirty-war-on-the-
national-health-service-review-john-pilger-documentary

16 www.stepforwardhomes.co.uk/rising-demand-affordable-homes-
veterans-cash-strapped-nhs-staff

17 www.telegraph.co.uk/news/uknews/8095160/London-firemen-
who-live-overseas.html

18 www.polfed.org/ranks/3277.aspx

19 https://homeofficemedia.blog.gov.uk/2017/09/12/police-welfare-
pay-and-wellbeing-september-2017

20 www.rcn.org.uk/professional-development/publications/pub-003303

21 www.nhsemployers.org/your-workforce/pay-and-reward/agenda-
for-change/pay-scales/annual

22 https://fullfact.org/economy/pay-rises-how-much-do-nurses-
police-teachers-and-mps-get-paid

23 https://webarchive.nationalarchives.gov.uk/20130320111101/
https://www.education.gov.uk/publications

24 https://assets.publishing.service.gov.uk/government/uploads/system/uploads/attachment_data/file/636389/School_teachers__pay_and_conditions_document_2017.pdf#page=19

25 www.liverpoolecho.co.uk/news/liverpool-news/how-much-binmen-merseyside-paid-13655277

26 www.expressandstar.com/news/2010/06/09/furious-binmen-set-to-take-strike-action

27 https://inews.co.uk/opinion/comment/crime-figures-police-officer

28 www.theguardian.com/uk-news/2018/aug/07/officers-second-jobs-police-federation-england-wales-survey

29 www.personneltoday.com/hr/public-sector-pension-reforms-ruling-supreme-court-fire-service-judges

4 Strugglers: The Boy Who Missed His Mother's Funeral

1 www.jrf.org.uk/report/destitution-uk-2018

2 www.trusselltrust.org/oxford-university-report

3 https://capuk.org/downloads/policy_and_government/Powerless-People-FINAL.pdf

4 www.ifs.org.uk/publications/14109

5 www.ippr.org/files/2019-06/public-health-and-prevention-june19.pdf

6 www.ippr.org/files/2019-06/public-health-and-prevention-june19.pdf

7 www.libertyhumanrights.org.uk/campaigning/stand-against-councils-punishing-poverty; http://manifestoclub.info/wp-content/uploads/2019/04/FOI-PSPO-fines-data.pdf; http://manifestoclub.info/pspos-the-busybodies-charter-in-2018

8 https://metro.co.uk/2019/10/09/mum-dying-brain-cancer-no-longer-enough-pip-payments-10885092

9 https://publications.parliament.uk/pa/cm201919/cmselect/cmworpen/83/8302.htm

10 www.changing-lives.org.uk

11 www.theguardian.com/society/2019/jun/05/austeristy-forcing-disabled-women-into-sex-work; https://publications.parliament.uk/pa/cm201719/cmselect/cmworpen/1166/1166.pdf

12 www.parliament.uk/business/committees/committees-a-z/
commons-select/public-accounts-committee/news-parliament-2017/
universal-credit-17-19

13 https://welfareweekly.com/nearly-half-of-dwp-staff-are-dependent-
on-benefits-to-make-ends-meet

14 www.ifs.org.uk/publications/14083

15 www.gov.uk/government/publications/universal-credit-29-april-
2013-to-10-october-2019/universal-credit-statistics-29-april-
2013-to-10-october-2019#introduction

16 Those who earn an average salary of £50,000 over a 43-year career will
contribute £219,039 to state welfare and pension spending. They would
have to receive the state pension for 38 years to become a net beneficiary.
The same person would also make a lifetime contribution of nearly
£110,000 to the health service.

Someone earning an average of £100,000 annually would contribute
almost £550,000 to the welfare system.

HM Revenue and Customs is preparing to send detailed statements
to millions of Britons next year showing how their tax is spent.
Today's analysis by the *Daily Telegraph*, the first of its kind, is based on
the formulas that will be used to compile the statements.
www.telegraph.co.uk/news/politics/10106437/Revealed-how-
much-you-pay-towards-benefit-bill.html;

good examples here of benefits spending: www.theguardian.com/
news/datablog/2013/jan/08/uk-benefit-welfare-spending; very good
up to date assessment: www.bbc.co.uk/news/business-47623277

5 Workers: The Mortician Who Became a Hairdresser

1 www.livingwage.org.uk/news/low-pay-spotlight-public-sector

2 Some unscrupulous lenders deliberately target customers who are
unable to pay back the loan.

3 Financial Ombudsman Service annual report 2019

4 www.theguardian.com/commentisfree/2019/dec/05/uber-loan-
program-debt

5 In the 3 months to September 2019

6   www.vice.com/en_us/article/z43kz5/amazon-warehouse-workers-have-resorted-to-sleeping-in-tents

7   www.jrf.org.uk/work/in-work-poverty; www.ifs.org.uk/uploads/WP201912.pdf

8   www.newstatesman.com/politics/economy/2019/11/real-reason-uk-s-record-employment-we-re-poorer

9   BBC Two *Newsnight*, 3 June 2019

10 www.frankfield.co.uk/latest-news/articles/news.aspx?p=1021661

11 www.theguardian.com/society/2019/nov/23/million-families-cut-universal-credit-benefits-debts

12 www.tuc.org.uk/blogs/our-broken-economy-has-locked-millions-workers-poverty-heres-how-fix-it

13 www.theguardian.com/books/2018/may/25/bullshit-jobs-a-theory-by-david-graeber-review

6 Renters: The Princess and the Paupers

1   www.rsnonline.org.uk/whitehall-updates-the-index-of-multiple-deprivation

2   www.bbc.co.uk/news/uk-england-49890749

3   www.housing.org.uk/press/press-releases/housing-benefit-freeze-9-in-10-homes-unaffordable-for-families; www.thisismoney.co.uk/money/buytolet/article-7885227/Government-set-end-housing-benefit-freeze-landlords-warn-moves-dont-far-enough.html

4   www.theguardian.com/society/2019/dec/26/rough-sleeper-gives-birth-to-twins-outside-cambridge-university

5   https://assets.publishing.service.gov.uk/government/uploads/system/uploads/attachment_data/file/852953/Statutory_Homelessness_Statistical_Release_Apr-Jun_2019.pdf

6   www.housing.org.uk/resources/people-in-housing-need

7   www.ifs.org.uk/publications/13471

8   www.resolutionfoundation.org/publications/inequality-street

9   www.resolutionfoundation.org/comment/two-housing-crises

10 www.resolutionfoundation.org/publications/game-of-homes-the-rise-of-multiple-property-ownership-in-great-britain

11 Guy Shrubsole, *Who Owns England? How We Lost Our Green and Pleasant Land, and How to Take It Back* (Glasgow: William Collins, 2019).
12 Speech to the Human Rights Council, 1 March 2017. www.ohchr.org/en/NewsEvents/Pages/DisplayNews. aspx?NewsID=21264&LangID=E

7 Millennials: The Travel Agent Who Swapped His Career for a Windsurfer

1 www.tuc.org.uk/news/ more-1-million-workers-will-be-work-christmas-day-says-tuc
2 www.ifs.org.uk/uploads/publications/bns/bn187.pdf; www.bbc. co.uk/news/business-37508968
3 www.ons.gov.uk/employmentandlabourmarket/ peopleinwork/employmentandemployeetypes/articles/ graduatesintheuklabourmarket/2017
4 www.theguardian.com/business/2019/jun/28/ gig-economy-in-britain-doubles-accounting-for-47-million-workers
5 www.gmb.org.uk/news/revealed-scandal-30000-nhs-workers-zero-hours-contracts
6 www.tuc.org.uk/blogs/uk-firms-used-18-million-zero-hour-contracts-2017-its-time-ban-zero-hour-contracts
7 www.resolutionfoundation.org/publications/irregular-payments
8 www.ipsos.com/ipsos-mori/en-uk/how-britain-voted-2019-election
9 https://victimsofcommunism.org/wp-content/uploads/2019/05/ VOC-2018-Annual-Report.pdf

8 Grafters: The City Trader Who Lied About His Holidays

1 www.rcplondon.ac.uk/news/doctor-can-growing-deprived-area-didn-t-stop-me-pursuing-my-dream-doctor
2 https://twitter.com/DrAsifOfficial; www.hulldailymail.co.uk/news/ uk-world-news/question-time-man-80k-twitter-3584811

3　www.medscape.com/
slideshow/2019-uk-doctors-salary-report-6011623#2

4　www.bma.org.uk/news/media-centre/press-releases/2019/february/
mps-pay-rise-will-leave-bitter-taste-for-nhs-workers-says-bma

9 Taxes: The Single Mother on Benefits Who Went to Prison and the Oligarch Who Didn't

1　(Woolcock) v Bridgend Magistrates' Court [2017] EWHC 34 (Admin)

2　(Woolcock) v Bridgend Magistrates' Court [2017] EWHC 34 (Admin)

3　www.thisismoney.co.uk/money/news/article-5105459/How-super-rich-London-pay-council-tax.html

4　www.theguardian.com/uk/2011/nov/26/one-hyde-park-council-tax

5　www.taxpayersalliance.com/council_tax_in_england_has_increased_by_57_per_cent_in_real_terms_in_20_years

6　www.citizensadvice.org.uk/about-us/how-citizens-advice-works/media/press-releases/harsh-collection-methods-adding-half-a-billion-in-fees-to-peoples-council-tax-debt-citizens-advice-reveals

7　www.citizensadvice.org.uk/about-us/how-citizens-advice-works/media/press-releases/harsh-collection-methods-adding-half-a-billion-in-fees-to-peoples-council-tax-debt-citizens-advice-reveals

8　www.ippr.org/files/2019-05/1559046258_a-poor-tax-reforming-council-tax-in-london-may2019.pdf

9　www.ifs.org.uk/publications/14566

10　www.ifs.org.uk/uploads/Presentations/Taxing%20couples.pdf

11　https://ifstudies.org/blog/taxing-families-in-the-uk

12　Cobham, A. and Janský, P. (2017). Global distribution of revenue loss from tax avoidance: re-estimation and country results. United Nations University, Wider Working Paper, p. 55.

13　www.theguardian.com/business/2019/nov/28/12-eu-states-reject-move-to-expose-companies-tax-avoidance

14　www.transparency.org.uk/uk-businesses-helping-worlds-corrupt-embed-themselves-british-establishment

15 Nicholas Shaxson, *The Finance Curse: How Global Finance is Making us All Poorer* (London: Grove Press, 2018).

16 www.equalitytrust.org.uk/wealth-tracker-18?platform=hootsuite; www.ons.gov.uk/peoplepopulationandcommunity/personaland-householdfinances/incomeandwealth/bulletins/wealthingreatbritainwave5/2014to2016#total-wealth

17 www.theguardian.com/business/2019/apr/03/inheritance-tax-loopholes-allowing-super-rich-to-pay-lower-rates

18 www.millionairesforhumanity.com

19 www.forbes.com/profile/jk-rowling/#14e594463aeb

20 www.forbes.com/profile/jk-rowling/#14e594463aeb

10 Born Poor: The Immigrant Who Wanted to be a Social Worker

1 www.ons.gov.uk/employmentandlabourmarket/peopleinwork/earningsandworkinghours/bulletins/genderpaygapintheuk/2019

2 www.ons.gov.uk/employmentandlabourmarket/peopleinwork/earningsandworkinghours/articles/ethnicitypaygapsingreatbritain/2018

3 https://publications.parliament.uk/pa/cm201617/cmselect/cmwomeq/89/89.pdf

4 https://publications.parliament.uk/pa/cm201617/cmselect/cmwomeq/89/89.pdf

5 Joseph Rowntree Foundation, Poverty and ethnicity: Balancing caring and earning for British Caribbean, Pakistani and Somali people, 2014; www.jrf.org.uk/report/caring-and-earning-among-low-income-caribbean-pakistani-and-somali-people

6 www.ons.gov.uk/employmentandlabourmarket/peopleinwork/employmentandemployeetypes/bulletins/regionallabourmarket/december2019

7 ONS report. www.thisismoney.co.uk/money/news/article-7759277/Total-household-net-wealth-surges-14trillion-stash-cash-pensions-property.html

8 www.ifs.org.uk/uploads/Presentations/The-characteristics-and-
   incomes-of-the-top-1-percent.pdf; www.economicshelp.org/
   blog/630/economics/economy-in-1980s

9 www.oxfam.org/en/why-majority-worlds-poor-are-women

10 www.oxfam.org/en/why-majority-worlds-poor-are-women

11 www.fawcettsociety.org.uk/news/the-fawcett-society-
   announces-date-of-equal-pay-day-2019

12 www.jrf.org.uk/report/
   supporting-ethnic-minority-young-people-education-work

13 Written submission by the Employment Related Services Association
   to the House of Commons Women and Equalities Committee,
   inquiry on employment opportunities for Muslims in the UK.
   https://publications.parliament.uk/pa/cm201617/cmselect/
   cmwomeq/89/89.pdf

14 This 2019 research was carried out by data consultancy CACI, which
   claims to give more detailed figures than the Office for National
   Statistics by analysing life expectancy on a 'granular' level. The data
   were derived from more than a million anonymised pension records,
   together with ONS mortality statistics.

15 www.kingsfund.org.uk/publications/whats-happening-life-
   expectancy-uk

16 www.theguardian.com/society/2019/apr/19/newborn-baby-deaths-
   may-be-on-rise-among-poorest-in-england

17 www.kingsfund.org.uk/publications/whats-happening-life-
   expectancy-uk

18 www.gov.uk/government/publications/the-long-shadow-of-
   deprivation-differences-in-opportunities

19 Bill Bishop, *The Big Sort: Why the Clustering of Like-Minded America Is
   Tearing Us Apart* (Boston: Mariner Books, 2009).

20 www.cer.eu/publications/archive/policy-brief/2019/
   big-european-sort-diverging-fortunes-europes-regions

11 Borrowers: The Railway Engine Mechanic Who Lost Her Job and Never Recovered

1 www.ncbi.nlm.nih.gov/m/pubmed/21463069
2 www.rcpsych.ac.uk/mental-health/problems-disorders/debt-and-mental-health
3 www.nationaldebtline.org/EW/sampleletters/Pages/Write-off-the-debt-%28sole-name%29.aspx
4 www.stepchange.org/debt-info/debt-and-mental-health-evidence-form.aspx
5 www.england.nhs.uk/south/info-professional/safe-use-of-controlled-drugs/opioids
6 www.thelancet.com/journals/lanpsy/article/PIIS2215-0366(18)30471-1/fulltext
7 www.bbc.co.uk/news/uk-50989633
8 The figures do not include outstanding mortgage debts but do include student loans. www.tuc.org.uk/news/broken-economy-driving-record-levels-household-debt-warns-tuc-0
9 www.nao.org.uk/wp-content/uploads/2018/09/Tackling-problem-debt-Summary.pdf
10 www.tuc.org.uk/news/broken-economy-driving-record-levels-household-debt-warns-tuc-0
11 www.gov.uk/government/statistics/company-insolvency-statistics-october-to-december-2019
12 www.theguardian.com/money/2019/oct/30/personal-insolvency-levels-approaching-highest-in-a-decade
13 www.bbc.co.uk/news/business-45302629
14 www.taxpayersalliance.com/cost_overruns_of_major_government_projects
15 www.ons.gov.uk/economy/governmentpublicsectorandtaxes/publicspending/bulletins/ukgovernmentdebtanddeficitforeurostatmaast/june2019#main-points
16 www.ons.gov.uk/economy/governmentpublicsectorandtaxes/publicsectorfinance/bulletins/publicsectorfinances/july2020
17 http://pubdocs.worldbank.org/en/753591576617452440/Debt-Overview.pdf

18 www.imf.org/en/Publications/WEO/Issues/2019/10/01/world-economic-outlook-october-2019; http://pubdocs.worldbank.org/en/753591576617452440/Debt-Overview.pdf; https://foreignpolicy.com/2019/12/31/global-economy-2020-outlook-positive-china-debt-trade-growth

19 www.nao.org.uk/wp-content/uploads/2020/09/The-production-and-distribution-of-cash.pdf

12 Strivers: The £90,000 Lawyer Who Didn't Feel Very Rich

1 Interview with the author, January 2020

2 www.telegraph.co.uk/news/newstopics/mps-expenses/11026474/Mark-Simmonds-Expenses-system-gave-Foreign-Office-minister-a-500000-lift.html

3 www.bbc.co.uk/news/uk-politics-28737781

4 www.dannydorling.org/books/onepercent/Material_files/DailyMail.pdf

5 www.oecd.org/unitedkingdom/Middle-class-2019-United-Kingdom.pdf

6 www.resolutionfoundation.org/publications/who-owns-all-the-pie; www.resolutionfoundation.org/app/uploads/2019/12/Who-owns-all-the-pie.pdf

7 www.heraldscotland.com/news/18217693.scottish-budget-third-scots-now-paying-taxes-higher-rates

8 In the UK a two-person household needs between £1,711 and £4,561 per month (after tax) to be in the middle-income class. Today 58 percent of the population is in this earning bracket, while 30 percent are in the lower-income class and 11 percent are in the upper-income class. On average, across OECD countries, 61 percent are in the middle-income class, 30 percent are in the lower-income class and 9 percent are in the upper-income class. Between the mid-2000s and mid-2010s in the UK the share of the population in the middle-income class has increased by 2.8 percent. More people than

ever may be able to call themselves middle-class earners but very few of them are feeling any richer.

9 https://read.oecd-ilibrary.org/social-issues-migration-health/under-pressure-the-squeezed-middle-class_689afed1-en#page1; www.oecd.org/els/soc/OECD-middle-class-2019-summary-flyer.pdf

10 www.bbc.co.uk/programmes/m0006740; also see Verkaik report at www.byfieldconsultancy.com/wp-content/uploads/From-Recruitment-to-Robots.pdf

11 www.brookings.edu/blog/future-development/2018/09/27/a-global-tipping-point-half-the-world-is-now-middle-class-or-wealthier

13 Savers: The Sailor and the Dinner Lady Who Ran Out of Money Before They Died

1 Beveridge, William. Social Insurance and Allied Services Report. Published by His Majesty's Stationery Office, November, 1942.

2 www.ifs.org.uk/bns/bn105.pdf

3 www.ageuk.org.uk/Documents/EN-GB/Campaigns/end-pensioner-poverty/how_we_can_end_pensioner_poverty_campaign_report.pdf?epslanguage=en-GB?dtrk=true

4 www.jrf.org.uk/data/pensioner-poverty

5 www.spi.ox.ac.uk/article/uk-pension-system-leads-to-sharp-increase-in-poverty-amongst-the-elderly

6 www.which.co.uk/money/pensions-and-retirement/options-for-cashing-in-your-pensions/annuities/annuity-rates-aly8c2z86kds

7 www.if.org.uk/the-issue

8 www.if.org.uk/research-posts/the-soaring-costs-of-government-pensions

9 www.centreforsocialjustice.org.uk/core/wp-content/uploads/2019/08/CSJJ7421-Ageing-Report-190815-WEB.pdf

14 Traders: The Day the Bookshop Didn't Sell Any Books

1 www.petersfieldpost.co.uk/article.cfm?id=118863&headline=Owner percent20haspercent20no

2 www.thebookseller.com/news/growth-bookshops-record-number-shops-disappear-high-street-985381

3 https://brc.org.uk/news/2019/worst-year-on-record-for-retail

4 www.theguardian.com/cities/ng-interactive/2019/jan/30/high-street-crisis-town-centres-lose-8-of-shops-in-five-years

5 www.uhy-uk.com/news-events/news/losses-at-top-100-uk-restaurant-groups-increase-to-93m-in-the-last-year

6 www.retailresearch.org/retail-crisis.html

7 www.tuc.org.uk/news/two-million-self-employed-adults-earn-less-minimum-wage

8 www.tuc.org.uk/news/two-million-self-employed-adults-earn-less-minimum-wage

9 www.ted.com/talks/paul_piff_does_money_make_you_mean/transcript?language=en#t-274710

10 https://arxiv.org/pdf/1802.07068v2.pdf

11 Simon C. Parker, *The Economics of Entrepreneurship* (Cambridge: Cambridge University Press, 2018).

12 www.telegraph.co.uk/money/consumer-affairs/easy-credit-hard-times-10-fold-rise-young-people-entering-insolvency

15 The City: The Classic-Car Enthusiast Who Forgot What Kind of Car His Broker was Driving

1 www.gov.uk/tax-on-dividends

2 www.ft.com/content/fdeb41ee-e079-11e9-b8e0-026e07cbe5b4

3 In 1986 face-to-face dealing of the trading floors of the City of London became computerised. Overnight the Big Bang created 1,500 millionaires. Some 95% of the firms had been owned by partnerships and, dazzled by the massive sums on offer, many simply sold up and retired.

4   Michael Lewis, *Flash Boys: A Wall Street Revolt* (New York: W. W. Norton, 2015), p. 98.

5   House of Commons Committee on Exiting the European Union, Asset Management Sector Report, 1 November 2017; see also https://assets.publishing.service.gov.uk/government/uploads/system/uploads/attachment_data/file/665668/The_Investment_Management_Strategy_II.pdf.

6   www.ft.com/content/93f7532a-786d-11e7-90c0-90a9d1bc9691

7   www.onlondon.co.uk/how-many-people-work-in-london-financial-services-and-what-do-they-do

8   www.theguardian.com/business/2011/dec/17/treasury-warned-over-traders-fees

9   www.theguardian.com/money/2016/jun/18/fund-managers-huge-fees-city-of-london-wall-street

10 www.telegraph.co.uk/finance/personalfinance/investing/11852003/The-City-serves-only-itself.-This-is-how-it-could-serve-us-all.html

11 www.prospectmagazine.co.uk/magazine/is-the-city-worth-it

12 www.telegraph.co.uk/finance/personalfinance/investing/11852003/The-City-serves-only-itself.-This-is-how-it-could-serve-us-all.html

13 John Kenneth Galbraith, *Money: Whence It Came, Where It Went* (Boston: Houghton Mifflin Harcourt, 1975), p. 5.

16 Wealth: The World-Famous Mountaineer Who Sleeps in His Ford Mondeo

1   www.fourfourtwo.com/features/why-do-so-many-footballers-end-broke-fourfourtwo-investigates

2   https://vault.si.com/vault/2009/03/23/how-and-why-athletes-go-broke

3   www.sec.gov/fast-answers/answersponzihtm.html

4   www.bbc.co.uk/programmes/m000cys7

5   Robert Verkaik, 'Are you being scammed?', *The i* newspaper, 2 September 2019.

17 Winners: The Numismatist Who Accidentally Cornered the Market

1 Although PFIs first came into being under John Major, they were hardly used.

2 www.ippr.org/news-and-media/press-releases/nhs-hospitals-under-strain-over-80bn-pfi-bill-for-just-13bn-of-actual-investment-finds-ippr

3 www.oxfam.org/en/press-releases/billionaire-fortunes-grew-25-billion-day-last-year-poorest-saw-their-wealth-fall

4 www.bbc.co.uk/news/business-51222675

5 www.forbes.com/profile/david-rubenstein/#44033108792f

6 www.forbes.com/profile/jamie-dimon/#375811145063

7 www.forbes.com/profile/stephen-schwarzman/#a2af1b0234a2

8 https://realinvestmentadvice.com/asset-bubbles-are-making-davos-billionaires-richer

9 https://content.knightfrank.com/resources/knightfrank.com/wealthreport/2019/the-wealth-report-2019.pdf

10 Scott Hankins, Mark Hoekstra and Paige Marta Skiba, 'The Ticket to Easy Street? The Financial Consequences of Winning the Lottery', The President and Fellows of Harvard College and the Massachusetts Institute of Technology, *Review of Economics and Statistics,* Vol. 93, Issue 3, August 2011, pp. 961–9. [Online]. (URL www.mitpressjournals.org/doi/abs/10.1162/REST_a_00114#.VpLMM1J327Q). (Accessed 8 September 2020).

11 www.epi.org/publication/state-of-american-wages-2018

12 www.suttontrust.com/wp-content/uploads/2020/01/pathwaystobankingreport-24-jan-2014.pdf

13 https://assets.publishing.service.gov.uk/government/uploads/system/uploads/attachment_data/file/549994/Socio-economic_diversity_in_life_sciences_and_investment_banking.pdf

14 https://content.knightfrank.com/content/pdfs/global/the-wealth-report-2020.pdf

15 https://content.knightfrank.com/content/pdfs/global/the-wealth-report-2020.pdf

18 Generation Poor: The Graduate Who Didn't Want to Move to London

1 www.gov.uk/government/news/
graduates-continue-to-benefit-with-higher-earnings
2 www.ons.gov.uk/economy/nationalaccounts/
uksectoraccounts/compendium/economicreview/april2019/
overeducationandhourlywagesintheuklabourmarket2006to2017
3 House of Commons Briefing Paper Number 1079, 28 June 2019,
Student Loans Statistics.
4 www.moneysavingexpert.com/students/repay-post-2012-
student-loan
5 www.suttontrust.com/our-research/uk-elites-pulling-away
6 www.smf.co.uk/press-release-class-ceiling-costs-working-class-
graduates-1700-new-research
7 www.ifs.org.uk/publications/7421
8 David Willetts, *The Pinch: How the Baby Boomers Took Their Children's
Future – And Why They Should Give it Back* (London: Atlantic Books,
2011), p. 1.
9 www.resolutionfoundation.org/press-releases/young-millennials-
are-being-short-changed-by-the-state
10 www.creditstrategy.co.uk/news/news-top-stories/ccjs-hit-highest-
peak-on-record-6788?utm_source=newsletter&utm_medium=
email&utm_campaign=CS%20%2D%20Newsletter
11 www.gov.uk/government/news/monitoring-social-mobility-
2013-to-2020
12 https://foodfoundation.org.uk/demand-for-free-school-meals-rises-
sharply-as-the-economic-impact-of-covid-19-on-families-bites/

19 Coronavirus: The Man Who Tried to Buy Some Toilet Paper

1 www.ons.gov.uk/peoplepopulationandcommunity/
birthsdeathsandmarriages/deaths/bulletins/
deathsinvolvingcovid19bylocalareasanddeprivation/
deathsoccurringbetween1marchand17april

2   The Reith Lectures 2020: Mark Carney, 'How We Get What We Value', 16 December 2012

3   www.mirror.co.uk/news/uk-news/nhs-faces-fresh-crisis-250000-22416470

4   www.nao.org.uk/wp-content/uploads/2020/11/Investigation-into-government-procurement-during-the-COVID-19-pandemic.pdf

5   https://citywire.co.uk/wealth-manager/news/odey-makes-115m-in-coronavirus-crash/a1339044

6   *Sunday Times*, 24 October 2020, p. 1.

7   www.instituteofhealthequity.org/resources-reports/build-back-fairer-the-covid-19-marmot-review

8   www.resolutionfoundation.org/publications/the-effects-of-the-coronavirus-crisis-on-workers

9   www.bbc.co.uk/news/business-53654712

10   www.resolutionfoundation.org/publications/young-workers-in-the-coronavirus-crisis

11   www.resolutionfoundation.org/app/uploads/2020/05/This-time-is-different.pdf

12   www.resolutionfoundation.org/publications/this-time-is-different-universal-credits-first-recession

13   www.bbc.co.uk/news/av/uk-52111389/coronavirus-minimum-wage-heroes

14   Danny Dorling, *Slowdown: The End of the Great Acceleration – and Why It's Good for the Planet, the Economy, and Our Lives* (New Haven: Yale University Press, 2020).

20 Enriching Our Society: How We All Get Rich

1   www.bankofengland.co.uk/knowledgebank/how-has-growth-changed-over-time

2   A decade of minus 1 percent interest rates has decimated savings.

3   https://fullfact.org/economy/uk-sixth-or-ninth-richest-country

4   https://fullfact.org/economy/poverty-uk-guide-facts-and-figures

5   https://socialmetricscommission.org.uk/wp-content/uploads/2020/06/Measuring-Poverty-2020-Web.pdf. The number of

children growing up in relative poverty has increased by 600,000 since
2012 (www.gov.uk/government/news/monitoring-social-mobility-
2013-to-2020).There are also 200,000 more people (2 million in
total) classified as too sick to work than when these records were first
recorded in 1993 (www.ons.gov.uk/employmentandlabourmarket/
peoplenotinwork/economicinactivity/timeseries/lf69/lms).

6 We may have reached peak employment for women. Peak employment for women has been driven by 'WASPI' (Women Against State
Pension Inequality) women, who had planned to retire at sixty but
were told they must work to sixty-five, and mothers who have been
forced to look for work to boost household income.

7 Yet the UK is ranked fifty-eighth in the world in terms of
economic gender equality. www.ons.gov.uk/employmentandlabour-
market/peopleinwork/employmentandemployeetypes/bulletins/
employmentintheuk/february2020

8 www3.weforum.org/docs/WEF_GGGR_2020.pdf

9 https://assets.publishing.service.gov.uk/government/uploads/system/
uploads/attachment_data/file/861444/House_Building_Release_
September_2019.pdf

10 https://www.ons.gov.uk/peoplepopulationandcommunity/
birthsdeathsandmarriages/deaths/bulletins/deathsofhomelesspeoplein
englandandwales/2019registrations

11 https://thecorrespondent.com/177/the-biggest-story-in-the-uk-is-
not-brexit-its-life-expectancy/23433342405-302f1fdb

12 www.theguardian.com/money/2019/aug/13/
danish-bank-launches-worlds-first-negative-interest-rate-mortgage

13 www.equalitytrust.org.uk/news/uk%E2%80%99s-five-richest-
families-now-own-more-wealth-bottom-13-million-people

14 Daniel Markovits, *The Meritocracy Trap: How America's Foundational
Myth Feeds Inequality, Dismantles the Middle Class, and Devours the Elite*
(London: Penguin Press, 2019).

15 https://hbr.org/2006/12/extreme-jobs-the-dangerous-allure-
of-the-70-hour-workweek

16 www.theguardian.com/news/datablog/2016/feb/26/uk-more-
middle-class-than-working-class-2000-data

17 http://blogs.bath.ac.uk/iprblog/2019/07/01/whither-the-middle-class

18 www.brookings.edu/blog/future-development/2018/09/27/a-global-tipping-point-half-the-world-is-now-middle-class-or-wealthier

19 Interview with the author, January 2020

20 www.cer.eu/publications/archive/policy-brief/2019/big-european-sort-diverging-fortunes-europes-regions

21 Anna Killick, *Rigged: Understanding 'the Economy' in Brexit Britain* (Manchester: Manchester University Press, 2020).

22 www.gov.uk/government/news/the-long-shadow-of-deprivation

23 Today we like to think the nation is governed by a neoliberalism which favours privatisation and deregulation. But the truth is, the UK economy is already a command economy which relies on constant injections of cash and national infrastructure projects like HS2. At its reductionist core our economy is based on cheap jobs and low productivity. How is this so different from the economies of Russia or China?

24 In purchasing-power-parity dollars

25 www.oecd.org/dev/44457738.pdf

26 www.theguardian.com/business/2020/jun/01/top-business-leaders-call-on-boris-johnson-to-set-out-green-recovery-plan

27 www.imf.org/en/Publications/SPROLLs/world-economic-outlook-databases#sort=%40imfdate%20descending

28 www.bbc.co.uk/news/business-51278036

29 John Kenneth Galbraith, *American Capitalism: The Concept of Countervailing Power* (Boston: Houghlin Mifflin Harcourt, 1952).

30 For the first time in American history hundreds of thousands of immigrants returned to their native countries, and some native US citizens left for Canada, Australia and South Africa.

31 https://greennewdealgroup.org

32 https://neweconomics.org/campaigns/green-new-deal

33 https://greennewdealgroup.org/wp-content/uploads/2020/01/GND_Bill_Summary_V2-1.pdf

34 A universal basic income was first described in Sir Thomas More's *Utopia*, published in 1516.

35 www.utpjournals.press/doi/pdf/10.3138/cpp.37.3.283

36 http://julkaisut.valtioneuvosto.fi/bitstream/handle/10024/161361/ Report_The%20Basic%20Income%20Experiment%2020172018%20 in%20Finland.pdf?sequence=1&isAllowed=y

37 Mariana Mazzucato, *The Value of Everything* (London: Allen Lane, 2018); see also www.nature.com/articles/d41586-018-04534-1.

38 For many countries, including the US, China and the UK, there have been no net gains in GPI for several decades.

39 Charity Commission. https://assets.publishing.service.gov.uk/ government/uploads/system/uploads/attachment_data/file/814656/ Charity_Commission_Annual_Report_2019_2019.pdf

40 https://fullfact.org/news/ are-unpaid-carers-saving-taxpayer-119-billion

41 http://media.wix.com/ugd/80ea24_ edd136e3b72b07c93775906aee3dfa35.pdf

42 Richard Wilkinson and Kate Pickett, *The Spirit Level: Why More Equal Societies Almost Always Do Better* (London: Bloomsbury Publishing, 2009).

43 www.oecd.org/sdd/statistical-insights-trust-in-the-united-kingdom. htm

44 www.weforum.org/agenda/2018/07/ low-voter-turnout-increasing-household-income-may-help

45 www.weforum.org/agenda/2018/11/these-countries-have-some-of- the-highest-voter-turnout-in-the-world

46 www.oecd.org/sdd/statistical-insights-trust-in-the-united-kingdom. htm

INDEX